Gods & Heroes
of the Media Age

Gods & Heroes of the Media Age

From Captain Nemo to *The X-Files*

by
John David Ebert

© 2015 John David Ebert
All rights reserved

ISBN: 978-0-9854802-9-5

Post Egoism Media | Eugene, Oregon

Acknowledgements

Special thanks are due to the following individuals for their support and encouragement: Michael Aaron Kamins, JD Casten, Thomas Ebert, Darryl Cooper, John Lobell and Nick Sambrook.

Contents

Acknowledgements   5

Preface   11

Introduction to an Age of Media Transformations   15

First Media Transformation:
The Classic Adventure Novel

Captain Nemo   25

Second Media Transformation:
Pulp Fiction

Tarzan, Lord of the Apes   35

Zorro and the Birth of Los Angeles   51

The Maltese Falcon
& the Cosmology of San Francisco   67

Conan the Barbarian   83

Third Media Transformation: Radio

The Shadow   97

Fourth Media Transformation: The Comic Strip

Flash Gordon   107

Fifth Media Transformation: The Comic Book

On Superman and Batman   115

Sixth Media Transformation: The Comic Book Phase II, The Marvel Renaissance

The Fantastic Four   127

Spider-Man   139

Seventh Media Transformation: The Postwar Paperback Novel

James Bond   149

Eighth Media Transformation:
The Celluloid Hero

Mad Max — 167

Ninth Media Transformation:
Television

The X-Files — 179

Tenth Media Transformation:
Cable Television

Breaking Bad — 201

The Walking Dead — 207

Epilogue — 213

Endnotes — 219

Preface

The following is a book, not so much about superheroes, but about the kinds of heroes made possible by transformations of media. The twentieth century has perhaps seen more media transformations than in the entirety of human history since the dawn of those first mud-brick cities in ancient Mesopotamia five thousand years ago when the first media were simply clay vases painted with petroglyphs that soon migrated into the cuneiform signs incised onto wet clay tablets. The Egyptians, meanwhile, were painting red and black hieroglyphs onto papyrus scrolls, which the Greeks also used, although with the innovation of the phonetic alphabet, while the Romans, who also used the papyrus or vellum scroll, went on to invent the codex, that is to say, a book with a spine and pages, a format very much favored by Christians as opposed to Jews, who preferred to continue with the scrolls. Egyptian hieroglyphs became extinct by the end of the fourth century AD, but scrolls continued, in both papyrus (plant) and vellum (animal skin) form well on into the Middle Ages right beside the codex up until about the eleventh century, when the Arabs introduced paper into Spain, an art which they had learned from the Persians who, in turn had derived it from the Chinese. Paper was cheaper and easier to make than drying out animal skins and so the format of the illuminated manuscript continued right down to the fifteenth century when, around 1439 in Mainz, Germany one Johannes Gutenberg transformed a wine press into the first printing press. (Dionysus, as it were, into Apollo). The Arabs were engulfing Constantinople at just about the same time in 1453, chasing out refugee Greek monks carrying satchels full of manuscripts unknown to the West for centuries right into the waiting arms of Rome and Florence, where they were promptly translated and the Western Clearing of Being began to "light up" (with its idea of Being as "objectivity") while the Eastern world slowly began a process of darkening from which–if one may so without Orientalist bias–it has never recovered.

All these media transformations took place over thousands of years, and each of these media favored a particular kind of narrative hero: the incised lines of the Babylonian tablets, for example, might favor a Gilgamesh–the one who conquered death–while the calligraphy of Egyptian papyrus did not favor epic heroes so much as exemplary characters like The Eloquent Peasant or Sinuhe, the man who committed sins against *Ma'at* for leaving Egypt and living his life amongst the barbarian tribes of Palestine. There is something eternal and unchangeable about the deeds of Gilgamesh (perfect for baked tablets), and a sense of ephemerality and historical contingency about Sinuhe or the Eloquent Peasant. The Hindus, meanwhile, invented the five Pandava Brothers–the original Fantastic Five–simply by telling oral tales about them, while the Homeric epics, written down around 750 BC, were acts of commemoration of an age of giants when men capable of deeds like the Trojan War lived long before the time of Homer himself, who was looking backward at them and trying to capture and preserve them in writing.

The twentieth century media explosion–still ongoing, and apparently gaining force, as every day seems to yield yet another new gadget for one to contend with–has been prodigious, and it has made possible a gallery of heroes and superheroes of great diversity and richness. The following manuscript, written (on a laptop) over approximately nine years, upon which I worked off and on between projects, was meant as a sort of cultural archaeology of these heroes. The thesis of the book is that the gods have survived and live on precisely through these popular media which favor their survival, while in the mainstream literary tradition they have mostly died out. And certainly, their cults no longer function. The gods, as both Holderlin and Heidegger lamented, have absconded from us, but yet Heidegger–engaged in writing his *Contributions*–never bothered with popular culture, where he would have found them alive and well and still continuing to draw breath amongst us.

Thus, the following book is a chronicle of the survival of the gods–to echo Jean Seznec–and a report on their state and condition. Many more media transformations still await us, and indeed the very thought is cause for nausea, since one can already foresee a plague of Titans spewing forth from out of the microchips implanted into all these gadgets. One can only keep head above water for so long.

If anything, now there are too many media making too many competing demands for the media-user's attention and so it is getting harder and harder for one to focus amidst this welter of digital chaos and make commitments to specific media.

Find your patron god.

And stick with him.

Introduction

to an Age of Media Transformations

Every new medium not only restructures and scraps the existing environment of a particular society, but it also makes possible the emergence of new phyla of gods, heroes and characters which hatch from these new media like pods. Such protagonists have very specific characteristics that are delineated by the morphic contours of their respective media. The Greek discovery of the phonetic alphabet, for instance, made possible Socrates as a philosophical hero in the pages of Plato's writing. Oral traditions, likewise, made possible the emergence of characters–such as Achilles, who was in origin, most likely from oral media–who are prone to *physical* acts and violence to solve their problems. Indeed, many of the world's existing epics were based on oral storytelling traditions that were only written down later on, when they were on the verge of extinction, such as the Poetic Eddas, which were committed to writing in haste as Christianity closed down around it with its codes. It is not an accident that the Gospels were written down immediately after the Romans destroyed the Jewish Temple, or the Pyramid Texts in the Fifth Dynasty, when Old Kingdom Egypt was collapsing and the priests were abandoning their rites. Oral traditions favor not only violent characters but also iconic heroes that loom large in the memory with simple mnemonic devices such as "the wise Nestor" or "the wrathful Achilles."

The emergence of the novel–in its Northern European configuration, at least–is a print-based medium that favors solitary reading and linear thinking. Accordingly, the kinds of heroes that it made possible were introverted, moody, brooding characters like Julian Sorel or Raskolnikov. In *Ulysses*, Stephen Daedalus doesn't do much *acting*; instead, he spends the great majority of the narrative *thinking*. And the same goes for the narrator of *Remembrance of Things Past* or Hans Castorp in *The Magic Mountain*. Thus, the novel as a medium, which displaced the epic together with its mighty heroes of action, favors contemplation and lonely introverted characters.

Pulp fiction, on the other hand, which is the first of the media transformations discussed by this book (after the Classic Novel, that is, within the pages of which the earliest stirrings of those characters endowed with supernatural powers which led to the later creation of the superhero seem to have begun: i.e. the Invisible Man, Jekyll & Hyde, Captain Nemo, etc.) seems to have created a cultural ecology in which the action-adventure hero could flourish once again. For pulp fiction, by contrast with the novel, has a much more rapid metabolism: it must sell copies on a monthly basis and so it must devise simple plots with mechanisms that keep readers coming back for more. The action heroes that transmigrated to pulp fiction from the pages of Verne's and Haggard's adventure novels were undying and impossible to kill figures who had been resurrected out of ancient myth and legend in order to be worn as tribal masks by a corporate readership who could put on their favorite pulp fiction magazine as a sort of tribal signifier and take it off again, whether it was *Argosy, Weird Tales, Amazing Stories*, or what have you.

With the emergence of radio as a new medium beginning immediately after the First World War, one did not put on the tribal mask of a Tarzan or a John Carter, Warlord of Mars; instead, one sat in the darkness and became *surrounded* by an incorporeal presence like The Shadow, whose echoing laugh seemed to come from all directions simultaneously. The radio, unlike print, has an oral / acoustic bias that subliminally reactivates the tribal traditions of sitting around the campfire listening to the village elders recount myths and tales from the time of dead ancestors and the days of Origin. The Shadow may be all-encompassing, but the Lone Ranger comes at one out of the dark like a tribal ghost from the ancestral frontier past. That is why, unlike all other cowboy heroes, he must appear wearing a mask, for the mask is instantly connotative of the tribal god.

Movies, especially popular during the Depression era, are collective art forms that overpower one with huge, mythical images of giant humans drained of all color (at least, initially). The experience of going in to the theater recaptures that of the Paleolithic descent into the caves lit only by firelight as the procession of initiates files past in awe, gazing at the totemic herds of the night sky constellations looming down at them. Thus, the Depression era invention of the genre of noir–not the detective story, which is print based (and so with Dupin or Sherlock Holmes follows linear logic) and emerged in the pages of Poe and Wilkie Collins in the nineteenth century–the noir genre of the 1930s is infected by the black and white talkies of the Hollywood era of those days, the days of Nathanael West's *Day of the Locust* or John Fante's *Ask the Dust*. At the same time, Dashiell Hammett in San Francisco (in the 1920s) and Raymond Chandler in Los Angeles (in the 1930s) invented the noir genre nearly simultaneously and one has the impression, while reading their novels, that the stories themselves were imagined in black and white. Depression-era imagery is an era of shadows and light, a retrieval of Late Renaissance chiaroscuro transplanted from German Expressionist cinema to Hollywood and thence to the pages of the noir novel.

The comic strip, meanwhile, which had already been up and running by the end of the nineteenth century in the form of political cartoons that were then followed by various forms of social satire, favors a world of trickster figures and quick sketch artists, as it were. But the transplantation of the adventure hero from the pulps to the Sunday strips–Buck Rogers, for instance, began as a pulp fiction novel, then immediately became one of the first adventure strips right alongside Tarzan in 1929–worked so well because of the necessary iconic compression and brevity favored by the strips. The adventure hero is himself already a two-dimensional figure with no complexity to him whatsoever, but is rather a cipher, or a function like the x and y in algebra. Now he could become *visually* appealing–Tarzan was merely naked and so was Conan, more or less–by putting a color suit on him *a la* Flash Gordon or the Phantom and plugging him into simple adventures that merely required a few moments for the eye to glide across the panels and to read a few quick captions that always promised to resolve a situation the next day or the next week, but never did, because the trick of the strips was to keep the forward momentum going from one day to the next. There *is* no plot resolution in a comic strip.

The comic book, on the other hand, which emerged in the mid 1930s, demanded brief stories with a beginning, a middle and an end since they were, after all a type of "book." The early comic books of Superman and Batman were usually anthologies of two or three stories and they always resolved their plots, but never managed to bring any harm to their hero protagonists. Comic books were stories for kids or for those with short attention spans who had no interest in reading longer books of print which took days or even weeks to complete. And with Marvel's reinvention of the comic book in the 1960s, a whole new galaxy of superheroes came into being–perhaps under the visual-tactile influence of television–with a certain banalization process, since the heroes, like Spider Man or the Fantastic Four, were now much more like real life human beings. From DC, which dominated in the 1930s, to Marvel in the 1960s, the trajectory of the hero is a bit like the shift from the heroes of Sophocles–remote, tragic, idealized–to those of Euripides, who puts the common man into the costumes of the gods and heroes.

The paperback novel, meanwhile, which emerged at about the time of World War II, created "the portable hero" for a generation on the move: one could read the adventures of one's favorite hero–James Bond, let's say, or Travis McGee–in the airport lounge, or on the bus, or on the plane, or even in the back seat of a car going cross country. The paperback could fit into one's back pocket and it made possible the rise of genres with an unmistakably dromoscopic increase in speed: characters like James Bond or John D. McDonald's Travis McGee were themselves highly mobile, nomadic and always on the move. Hence, the paperbacks began to appear and soon to dominate the newsstands in "non-places" like drugstores, supermarkets and airports, places where people were always moving quickly through them, never lingering for long and always on the way to somewhere else.

With television, the miniaturization process of scaling down big Hollywood movies and inserting them into living rooms set the pattern for miniaturizing everything and everyone in the culture: the domestication of rock stars (Elvis Presley on Ed Sullivan), presidents (John F. Kennedy), and movie stars (such as Barbara Stanwyck, whose film career of the 1940s was scaled down for a televisual one on *The Big Valley*). Television is a low resolution medium that shrinks down and dismantles all icons and images into electronic ka's (to borrow an Egyptian term for the soul). But the shadow side of its increase in audience participation in social problems–one of McLuhan's favorite points–is also an increase in social paranoia. Invisible electromagnetic spectra could be anywhere and everywhere: hence the excavation of paranoia in a show like *The X-Files*, where hidden entities are constantly at work disrupting people's lives.

With cable television, commercials were–at least initially– removed, as were standards and practices, so it became possible to create a miniature movie theater for the first time for those who wanted a scale model, doll's house replica. The first characters to appear in the Cable Renaissance set up by HBO and Showtime–Tony Soprano, Al Swearengen (*Deadwood*), Nancy Botwin (*Weeds*)–were recycled from the televisual genres of the 1960s and crossed with the frankness and candor of the movies. In doing so, cable TV (while it lasted) was able to retrieve and domesticate the "dangerous narrative" which had once been the movie theater's inheritance of the avant-garde in the 1970s. The protagonists of the "dangerous narrative," whether in the movie theaters of the 1970s or on cable in the 2000s, were always characters involved in morally questionable activities. The viewer might not necessarily identify with them, but they were fascinating as probes dropped into unimaginably harrowing situations to find out what might happen to the characters, as the viewer, to his horror, watched these rock bottom descents from the safety and comfort of his living room.

And that is the span of media transformations covered in this book, from the Classic Novel of the 1870s to the Cable Renaissance of the 2000s. Currently, cable TV is in process of collapsing in on itself as it migrates to the Internet—a vast and terrifying new medium the potential of which for wrecking people's lives with hacking, porn addiction, copyright infringement and zombification has yet to be fathomed. But HBO has closed up shop and called it a day on cable and has now transmigrated to the Internet to rival Netflix, Hulu and Amazon Instant Video.

What new species of heroes will emerge out of *this* medium have yet to fully reveal themselves. But considering that the Internet bias for televisual watching encourages what is known as "binge watching," since entire seasons are normally made available all at once for the viewer as addict, the amount of time spent in front of the screen will most likely *increase* rather than decrease, eating up huge blocks of time that could be spent doing more constructive activities. Perhaps *The Walking Dead* got it right:

These shows are turning us all into zombies.

First Media Transformation:

The Classic Adventure Novel

Captain Nemo

"Then Captain Nemo seemed to grow enormously, his features to assume superhuman proportions..."
–Jules Verne, *20,000 Leagues Under the Sea*

Captain Nemo, who first appears in Jules Verne's 1870 novel *20,000 Leagues Under the Sea*, is Western literature's first gigantic human (the first, that is, since the various giants and trolls of Medieval literature were scaled down by Cervantes to their proper proportions in realistic, three dimensional space), and as such, signals the beginnings of that tendency in its literature to produce, over the ensuing decades, and with ever more and more frequency as it goes along, beings of superhuman proportions with superhuman powers, skills and mythical abilities. Indeed, Verne scales Nemo up to the size of a Medieval Christ Pantocrator precisely by scaling the earth down to the size of a mere plaything fit to be held in Nemo's palm, precisely as Christ in his mode as *Salvator Mundi* once held the earth in the palm of his left hand in the shape of a circle bisected by a "T." The "T" was not only a reference to the cross, but signified the division of the earth into the three continents of Europe and Africa (below the horizontal bar) and Asia (above it). All Western maps, in those days, were "oriented" toward the East, the direction of Jerusalem in relation to Europe (and also the rising sun), which often occupied the bull's eye centers of such "T and O" maps.

On one such map, the so-called Hereford Map of about 1285, the earth is surrounded by a thin aqueous ring (hence the "O") upon which the three continents have been represented with Jerusalem in the center and the east occupying the zone normally given today to the north. One notes that the prevailing characteristic of this map is that of the predominance of the element of earth over water, for the earth was still gigantic in those days, and the degree to which water predominates over its terrestrial surface was not yet known. But as the maps evolve over the years, not only does the aqueous element–as Peter Sloterdijk has shown[1]–increase, but the earth itself, as it is known, mapped and charted by its "discoverers," gradually shrinks.

In the Fra Mauro map of 1459, the earth is now properly oriented with Europe and Asia at the top and Africa at the bottom, while one notes the significant incursion onto the map of water. Earth still predominates, but the ratio between the two elements is already beginning to change. By the time of the Behaim globe (the West's first such three dimensional orb) in 1492, the date of Columbus's historic voyage, the ratio is about 50/50, for one side of the globe is composed mostly of the three traditional continents while the opposing side, where the Americas should be represented, is a huge semiotic vacancy filled in with ocean.

On Martin Waldseemuller's black and white planispheric 2D projection of 1507, (the map that gave America its name) the continents, despite the irruption of a thin wedge representing what was then known of America, are notably shrinking, while the world-surrounding ocean begins to engulf them. By the time of Mercator's projection of 1569, the continents which had once dominated in the early T and O maps have now receded to an almost miniature scale. And with the voyages of Captain Cook in the 1770s, who restlessly circumnavigated the globe, the earth has been encompassed and tyrannized over by the Western cartographical imagination. It is a mystery no more.

Captain Nemo is, of course, a sort of idealized distillation of these Western nautical heroes, and his effortless circumnavigation of the globe by submarine in Verne's novel underscores his epic achievements as having complete command over the planetary oceans. One has the impression, in reading the novel, that the planet is a mere plaything for him, just as it was, once upon a time, for Christ as *Salvator Mundi*. Verne, moreover, in ascribing god-like abilities to his protagonist, scales him up to mythical dimensions, while simultaneously flattening out the Western hero of the realistic novel to two dimensions. Nemo has far more in common with the heroes of the ancient epics like Sindbad and Odysseus–essentially compressed hieroglyphs of mythic deeds– than he does with complex introverted heroes of the Western novel like Julien Sorel or Wilhelm Meister, who spend much of the course of their narratives *thinking*.

That he represents a sort of industrial age equivalent of the Classical Roman god Neptune need hardly be argued. His refusal ever to set foot on land, and his hostility to men of civilization, reveals him as god of the aqueous element in disguise. Verne, furthermore, gives to him the power of Jupiter's mythical thunderbolt (Neptune's trident is, of course, an altered thunderbolt) in the form of the submarine's ability to emit electrical discharges against unwary natives. And Verne, in making him the first man ever to set foot on the South Pole, recalls the three legendary footsteps of the god Vishnu in his avatar as Vamana the dwarf, each of whose footsteps becomes gradually larger until he circumscribes the known cosmos.

But it is in his character as Opener of the Way that Nemo becomes most evidently god-like in his powers. Midway through the novel Verne has the crew of the *Nautilus* traveling up the Red Sea, the legendary site of Moses' parting of the waters as the lord who Opens the Way, in this case, for the Hebrews. But Verne nods at the Moses myth by having Nemo deduce the existence of a so-called Arabian Tunnel beneath the isthmus of Suez (the canal was not yet quite completed) down to which he takes his crew, and which enables him to Open the Way between the Red Sea and the Mediterranean Ocean. (The epithet "Opener of the Way" was actually the name of an old Egyptian deity named Wepawet, the son of Anubis, a jackal-headed man who was able to open the way for the dead to travel down into the Egyptian underworld. It is possible that Moses usurps this attribute specifically from Wepawet as he Opens the Way *out* of Egypt as Underworld for the Hebrews to escape into the Promised Land).

But in any event, Captain Nemo's powers over the globe are considerable, and have the effect of elevating him to god-like status. In this respect, he is a two-dimensional character who represents a *function* like the *x* in an algebraic equation: namely, the image of the West's power over the globe as a mere plaything and toy for its predatory "discoverers" to devour, like Saturn eating his children. He is the archetypal Nautical Hero of Globalization Phase II, to borrow from Sloterdijk's analysis of the history of globalization in his book *In the World Interior of Capital*,[2] and as such, he represents the bifurcation point in the history of Western literature at which the hero of the Western novel evolves (or perhaps devolves) into the superhero, a figure of mere compression of iconic powers and mythical abilities into imagistic form. (Nemo's rise parallels that of the Graphic Revolution, in the form of what were then new media, such as comic strips, yellow backs, films and photographs).

The Western industrial superhero, then, comes onto the stage from out of the seas, following the genealogical branch that leads from Gulliver and Crusoe down through Arthur Gordon Pym and Ahab. He is, in origin, a nomad, representing the type of hero–a very old one, like Monkey in the Chinese epic *Journey to the West*–who is fundamentally hostile to the very order of civilization. Later characters such as Tarzan, the early Siegel and Shuster Superman of the 1930s, and the Hulk will follow in his wake as antagonists of the civilized order, embodiments of a superordinate power that cannot be trusted and must be carefully *excluded* from that order. His role in origin then, is not immunological but antigenic to the very idea of the city, like one of Deleuze and Guattari's nomads who stream across the smooth spaces of the deserts and plains where they encounter cities as merely unpleasant striations in the way of their transversal vectors.[3]

Nemo, whose name is Latin for "no man" (since he is not a man, but a god in disguise) is even associated with a totem animal, the Nautilus, after which his submarine is named for its principle of armoring itself within the shell of an exoskeleton. Nemo usurps technology, that is to say, not for the purpose of bettering or advancing civilization along the lines of its Progress metanarrative, but for constructing a private shell of invulnerability around himself with which he is able to make his own world, like an astronaut in outer space. Nemo "nomadizes" technology, reterritorializing it as a war machine at odds with the state apparatus. Inside of it, he is invulnerable and arm(or)ed, a one man army like Batman. Nemo inside of his submarine-as-singularity (not yet mass produced) is like an evolutionary regression back to one of those ancient Placoderms, bony-plated armored fish from the Devonian who appropriated the exoskeletal techniques of the crustaceans (temporarily at least) to defend themselves against predation.

But the fish, as in the case of Christ, is an ancient embryonic symbol for "birth," and so Captain Nemo becomes for us the embryo which will soon unfold and differentiate itself topologically into the Cambrian explosion of the universe of superhero phyla in which we now find ourselves living.

Second Media Transformation:
Pulp Fiction

Tarzan, Lord of the Apes

Origins

When we go in quest of origins, we often find ourselves inside the primordial darkness of caves. There is, for instance, something cavern-like–even vaginal–about the singularity that gave rise to the Big Bang. Human art, too, seems to have begun in a cave some 30,000 years ago in Chauvet, France, where we find the first recorded paintings, in this case of felines and horses. Buddhist art, likewise, begins in caves where stupas were hewn into the living rock at places like Bhaja or Karli in India. Islam also emerged out of a cave, and in a way, European art too hatched out of the cavern cosmology bequeathed to it by Islam and the Byzantine world, as a study of the evolution of Annunciation paintings demonstrates. The movie theater, in addition, grew out of the Arabic theory of optics, with its idea of the human eye as a sort of miniature cavern, just like a mosque, into which light rays were thought to penetrate. This idea led to the invention of the *camera obscura* (Latin for "dark room") and the rest, as they say, is history.

In tracing the origins of the mediatic superhero, we find ourselves, once again, inside a cave, in this case, a cave located in the Arizona desert, of all places. For that is where the hero of Edgar Rice Burroughs' first novel *A Princess of Mars* (1912) finds himself in the opening chapter, after having been chased up a mountain by a group of pursuing Apache Indians. Once inside the cave, Carter believes himself safe, but soon, he realizes that his astral body has separated from his physical body, which he sees lying on the floor of the cave beneath him. In a few moments, he finds himself looking up into the desert sky at the red star of Mars, and is immediately transported to that planet as though by means of a shamanic vision.

As the narrative progresses, John Carter's status as the prototype of the comic book superhero is immediately confirmed, for he finds that upon Mars he can jump enormous distances since he carries within him the mass and laws of the Earth, a planet that is larger and more gravitationally dense than Mars. He is also capable of supreme feats of strength and agility and is more powerful generally than anyone else on Mars. Thus, John Carter, once transported to Mars, finds himself in possession of superpowers and is, so far as I know, the first character in the history of Euro–American literature to do so.[4] Carter's powers, furthermore, are similar to those later ascribed to Superman, a character whose abilities likewise derive from the fact of his coming to earth from another planet with different laws, laws which render him invulnerable to just about everything. In his first appearances in *Action Comics* during the late 1930s, he too began by jumping over vast distances, for it took several issues over the course of several years before Superman learned how to fly.

Superman, then, is the direct lineal descendant of John Carter, Warlord of Mars. Both characters are beings who have descended to their respective planets from the heavens above (Burroughs' Mars is really just a metaphor for Earth during the Bronze Age) and both, therefore, are variations of the archetype of the advent of the Wonder Child from the Sky Father, since the sky, in ancient myth is normally (though not always) assigned a masculine valency.[5]

John Carter's superpowers, it should be noted, arise out of a discontinuity, for he is a figure taken from the context of one world and thrust into another with different laws from his own, and this contextual displacement is the cause of those powers. In other words, he creates his own space with its own laws and is therefore a sort of world unto himself, for he is completely at odds with his Martian surroundings. (A similar phenomenon applies to Tarzan as well, for in the context of the jungle, his powers seem to blend naturally with his surroundings, but when Burroughs removes him from the jungle and places him in the streets of Paris, his great strength and gymnastic skills make him seem larger than life). This scenario is not unlike the idea of moving frames of reference in Einsteinian physics, in which each object is regarded as having created its own independent spacetime, especially as it approaches light speed.

John Carter and Tarzan, moreover,–and indeed, all later superheroes–exist in a world that is no longer that of the perspectival space of European painting and Newtonian physics, in which objects were regarded as inhabiting the same overall spatial container, for the universes of Relativity and of the superhero are actually that of the older, more ancient realm of *audile-tactile space*, the space configured by the ear together with the sense of touch, not that of the eye (for whereas the eye creates a visual continuum, the sense of touch is inherently discontinuous). In the highly tactile artwork of Paleolithic man, for example, each painted or carved animal existed in its own space entirely independently of all the other animals represented on the cave walls nearby: this is why we find the animals traced over each other, or floating upside down or sideways. Each animal is pictured in the act of emerging from a spaceless, timeless Void, and not pictured as a unified herd on a plain grazing beneath the sun.

Acoustic space is also the world of pre-literate tribal man, a resonant dimension of masked apparitions and mythical figures which are best accessed via the sonically rhythmic techniques of shamanic drumming or Hindu mantras. Thus, it should come as no surprise to the reader of *A Princess of Mars* that the first beings which John Carter encounters upon Mars are giant green creatures with four arms who live 300 year life spans, for these are precisely the sorts of beings which we find in ancient myth: giants with multiple arms (like the Hundred Handed Ones in Hesiod, or almost any Tibetan bodhisattva) and figures like the pre-diluvial kings in the Bible who live for unusually long life spans.

Edgar Rice Burroughs' first novel, *A Princess of Mars*, is not only important for its invention of the kind of superhero that will later lead to the comic book superhero, but also for showing us that the world into which the West was then entering was precisely that patterned by the acoustic spaces of tribal man. Picasso's 1907 painting *Les Demoiselles d'Avignon* had already drawn its inspiration from the masked apparitions of African art, and so in the realms of both high and low culture a descent into the tribal world of acoustic space was going on simultaneously. And it is out of this tribal world that the masked apparitions of the superhero would eventually emerge, fully formed.

Burroughs was a kind of pop culture analogue of James Joyce, for just as Joyce had prophesied (in 1939) that all the tribal Finns would again awake in contemporary electric society, so Burroughs was concerned, in his pulp fiction narratives, with making visible the West's Viconian return into the Heroic Age of tribal man.[6] And no character was more exemplary of a return to the primitive than Burroughs' other great creation, Tarzan of the Apes.

Descent

If Edgar Rice Burroughs, with his earlier protagonist John Carter, Warlord of Mars, had in 1912 established the pattern of the superhero who arrives on the ground from the heavens above, then with his second creation–Tarzan, Lord of the Apes–he invented the idea of the superhero who emerges, Titan-like, from out of the earth itself. The narrative pattern in which Tarzan is raised by apes in Africa to become a literate, thinking man capable of walking the streets of Western cities is a disguised retelling of the Darwinian myth of human evolution from apes to civilization. For Tarzan, brought up amongst a tribe of African apes, is symbolically descended from *beings of the earth*, the same beings, no less, who have spent six or seven million years quietly constructing the human physical body beneath an enclosed canopy of African trees. By the time this body was ready, with Lucy and her people, to embark upon the traumas of the open savannah, it was simultaneously prepared for the descent of the human *soul* which took up its residence in this newly constructed body like a mother bird settling down to brood in her nest.[7]

Pearls

It is, however, also possible to look at the Tarzan narrative from a Gnostic point of view since the image of a man who has lost himself amongst the animals but yet gradually acquires the tools of language which allow him to recall his properly human self has something in common with Gnostic narratives like "The Hymn of the Pearl." In that story, a man is sent into Egypt (symbolic of the earth; the fallen world) by his parents in the East (the land of light and hence a stand-in for the heavens) in order to find a mysterious pearl (his soul) and bring it back. But once he has arrived in Egypt, he forgets his mission and begins to think and dress like the Egyptians (as Tarzan thinks and "dresses" amongst the apes). He has to be reminded of his cosmic mission by a herald who is sent down on behalf of the heavenly powers to help him (in this case, Tarzan's friend, the Frenchman D'Arnot, who teaches him how to speak), and once he remembers his true identity, he is able to slay the serpent and steal the pearl and return with it to his parent's abode (i.e. back to the heavens). Tarzan, likewise, having been raised by apes, is in the position of a being who has forgotten that he belongs to another world entirely (Europe, in this case), but he is reminded of who he really is–a rational, thinking being–once he discovers his parents' abandoned tree house where he teaches himself how to read. His acquisition of literacy sunders him from the animal realm, opening up a new world horizon of being-human in the Heideggerian sense, for he realizes that he is a being capable of greater (mental) feats than they and soon he rises amongst them to the commanding position of "Lord of the Apes" at the top of the animal hierarchy (the Gnostic kingly motif in disguise).

Icon

Tarzan is an iconic character whose essence consists in stripping him of all civilized encumbrances: he wears no clothing save a panther-skin loincloth and for weapons, carries only his father's hunting knife, and a bow and arrow.[8] Through having been raised in the jungle by apes, he has become incredibly strong and has learned amazing gymnastic feats by means of leaping from treetop to treetop. He has recovered abilities and instincts of the physical-animal body which have become atrophied by us moderns dwelling in the concrete and steel caverns of our metropolises. We take note that it is at precisely the moment when the skyscraper is growing like an iron tree out of the grimy concrete canyons of Chicago and New York that Tarzan hatches from out of the egg of folk culture as a counter image to this new urban apotheosis, for he embodied everything which the West was leaving behind in preparation for its ascent to the stars. In Merian C. Cooper's *King Kong* (1933), the ape is cast from the heights of a skyscraper and hurled out of the heavens to the earth below, like the Greek blacksmith god Hephaestus who was kicked from the sky and sent crashing to the island of Lemnos, for the antipathy between ape and city in that film parallels the solemn hatred of Tarzan of the Apes for the modern megalopolis. They are mutually exclusive principles.

Poliphobia

The crucial thing about Tarzan as a superhero–in many ways, the *first* superhero who will lead directly to the medium of the comics–is that *he is absolutely antithetical to civilization* (just as Captain Nemo was, as we have seen). In contrast to the superhero as later reinvented by Stan Lee and Jack Kirby during the 1960s, Tarzan is a poliphobic hero full of hatred at all things urban. As Burroughs himself remarked: "Perhaps the fact that I lived in Chicago and yet hated cities and crowds of people made me write my first Tarzan story..."[9]

The 1983 film version of the Tarzan story makes this antipathy between Tarzan and cities quite clear, for in *Greystoke: The Legend of Tarzan* the central point of the film is that Tarzan hates the city and loves only the jungle.

It might be worth pausing for a moment, though, to dwell on the film's glaring examples: the curtain opens on a primordial image of the jungle in which a distant volcano spews incandescent lava across a landscape riven with molten shafts of sunlight, like Frederic Edwin Church's 1862 painting of *Cotapaxi*, the

South American volcano. This image out of nineteenth century Romantic landscape painting points to the affiliation between Tarzan's poliphobia and the antipathy toward Industrialization evident in the Romantic sensibility generally.

The filmmakers then proceed to tell the story of Tarzan mostly as Burroughs has given it to us, only they have Tarzan's friend D'Arnot (played by Ian Holm), after being nearly killed by jungle natives and saved by Tarzan, teaching him how to read and write in addition to learning how to speak. (According to the original novel, Tarzan is raised by apes but he eventually teaches himself how to read when he finds books in his parents' abandoned tree house. Later, D'Arnot teaches him how to talk, but by this point Tarzan has already learned, through reading books, how to reason, and he has therefore liberated himself from a merely horizontal equation with his fellow animals. He is *more than* animal, even while preferring their company to that of other humans, for animals cannot think abstractly using concepts).

In the film, D'Arnot and Tarzan make their way toward civilization and as they move out of the African jungle, their first contact with anything resembling civilized society comes in the form of an ivory trading outpost. Here, the two are treated badly by the locals who suspect them of being criminals on the run, and while the men are on the verge of attacking D'Arnot, Tarzan leaps down from the rafters above and shouts "Fire!" while simultaneously tossing a gas lantern onto a tapestry which bursts into flames. Tarzan and D'Arnot flee, and as they climb back into their boat, the burning town is visible in the distance behind them. Thus, Tarzan's first encounter with civilization ends in its very destruction.

As the narrative progresses, Tarzan and D'Arnot eventually arrive at the Greystoke estate in England, where Tarzan is greeted warmly, despite still exhibiting many ape-like characteristics. Here, he meets and falls in love with Jane (in the novel, he encounters her in Africa, as the victim of a shipwreck). The filmmakers, interestingly, show him lingering about the rooftops of the estate, thereby indicating the inward relationship shared by his arboreal habitat with the later rooftop econiche of the comic book superhero whom he prefigures.

Through most of Burroughs' novels, Tarzan's perspective is from the treetops, where he looks down upon men in order to spy on them or else rescue them, for though he has emerged from the earth and belongs to the realm of the earth archetype, he is also a spirit being forever swooping down to catch and rescue the poor human soul who has fallen and become entangled upon the earthly plane below, like Superman forever plucking Lois Lane from one difficult situation after another. (Compare Cupid lifting up Psyche from the realm of her domestic drudgeries and carrying her to his rooftop castle).

In the film, meanwhile, Tarzan has a number of adventures in London that are mostly disappointing and humiliating to him, including an episode in which he discovers his ape father held captive as a lab specimen in a cage and sets him free so that the two can run about the streets of the city, eventually winding up in a tree, where the ape is shot and killed by a constable. Tarzan holds civilization accountable for the murder of his "father" and decides that he will have nothing more to do with it. In the film's closing scenes, we glimpse him frolicking once more amongst the apes in the jungles of Africa, while a fully clad Jane stands beside D'Arnot looking on with no evident intention of joining him.

Nomad

Historically, the nomad is a figure entirely at odds with cities. As Gilles Deleuze and Felix Guattari have written in their "Treatise on Nomadology," in their book *A Thousand Plateaus*,[10] the nomad travels across *smooth space* and represents a "war machine" perennially crashing into cities mostly because they happen to lie in his path. Cities, on the other hand, represent the world of *striated space*, for they disrupt the smooth and even flow of the vast plains across which the nomad moves. Wherever the nomad goes, he is primarily attempting to follow the contours of the world of his smooth space; cities merely get in the way of his accomplishing this task.[11]

Tarzan, too, is a loner and a nomad who prefers his own company. He calls the jungle his home, but he sleeps only in the trees and never stays in one place for very long.

In him, we become aware that the superhero begins as a type of retrieved Paleolithic hunter - nomad essentially *in opposition to the city as such*.

Castaway

Tarzan belongs to the genre of the castaway that began with Defoe's *Robinson Crusoe* in the eighteenth century and continues on through *Swiss Family Robinson* and Jules Verne's *The Mysterious Island* in the nineteenth (where Captain Nemo puts in a second appearance). The story of Tarzan, however, differs from all these other narratives in that Tarzan himself is a *second generation castaway* since his parents, the original castaways, are dead. Raised by apes, Tarzan has been cut off almost entirely–although not completely, for there is that tree house of his parents'–from his own society. In the case of those earlier Robinsonades–as the genre used to be known–the castaways normally attempt to rebuild a miniature version of Western civilization out of the scraps of seaspawn and seawrack immediately available to them (this remains true even of late and decadent examples of the genre such as Peter Weir's film *The Mosquito Coast* or Robert Zemeckis's *Castaway*). The point of such narratives seems to be that even if you take all his civilization away from him and cast him ashore upon an island, Western man is so aggressively inventive that he will spontaneously proceed to reconstruct that very same mechanical civilization even if he has to use cocoanuts for weights and palm fibers for pulleys. Tarzan's parents, with their tree house stuffed full of books and belongings, had likewise attempted to build a scale model of Western society.

Tarzan, however, differs from all of these castaways in that not only does he never attempt to recreate a miniature version of his own civilization (which would be familiar enough to him from the contents of the tree house) but *he actively disdains the very civilization which produced him.*

Giants

The years between 1914–18, the period of the Great War, as it has come to be known–and as Steven Spielberg in his movie *War Horse* has portrayed it–was an age of ever-gigantifying machines. The exaggerated size of these fabulous, mythical machines which appear on the covers of science magazines of that time such as *Electrical Experimenter* is in reality an index of their *psychological* effect upon the human mind and body of the time, but the images from these covers also show us that it was during the years of the Great War that society did indeed come under attack by its own machines in a war of almost Miltonic, cosmological magnitudes, exactly as H. G. Wells had prophesied in his *War of the Worlds* of 1898. Thus, the First World War was not so much a war of democrats vs. aristocrats, but *the first great war of humanity against its own machines.* The hyperbole of the images on these magazine covers effectively shows human beings engaged in desperate battle against gigantic mechanical killing machines, like the Imperial Walkers of *The Empire Strikes Back*. Note that it is *not* a vision of people fighting against people, as is the case with other images of battles past.

Thus, Tarzan appears larger than life for the primary reason that it was during the years of the Great War in which the machine achieved a sort of gigantifying apotheosis, for all kinds of new weapons of destruction were invented–flamethrowers, tanks, mustard gas, aeroplanes, etc.–which had the effect of tyrannizing over the puny human being and scaling him down to the size of an ant.

The problem of the superhero, then, is one of scale: when the human being disorients his own sensibilities through the production of bizarre and gigantic extensions of his own articulated anatomy in the form of terrifying machines, the imagination responds to this assault by enlarging the size and importance of the human being through attributing supernatural powers to him in the folkloric imagination of popular culture. Thus, Ant Man becomes Giant Man at precisely those moments in which he is most threatened by one or another of the villain's super-techno-gadgets.

Criminals

Now let's take a look at a particular scene from a Tarzan novel, *The Return of Tarzan*, in which Tarzan is walking alone one night in the streets of Paris when he hears a woman scream and he runs inside a building and rushes up a staircase into a room where he finds the woman being harassed by a group of men. He makes short work of the men, who all flee, but when the police arrive, the woman claims, to Tarzan's astonishment, that it was Tarzan who had broken into her room and tried to assault *her*.

The two policemen insist on taking Tarzan into custody, but he will have none of that and so beats them to a pulp and escapes through an open window out onto the Paris rooftops.

This scene occurs within the first few chapters of the second Tarzan novel, and we can already see it foreshadowing the coming development of the entire superhero mythos. Let us take note of the structural elements here which will later become prefabricated features of the superhero's universe: first, the image of the hero who rushes blindly to the aid of an anonymous cry of distress in a big city; then the scenario of the superhero who single handedly takes out a group of villains in close combat; but most importantly, the conflict between the hero and the police, for the function of the superhero is *not* an extension of the law, as is often wrongly assumed, sometimes even by the creators themselves.[12] His actions are those of a vigilante who by-passes due process and takes matters into his own hands: that is his whole *raison d'etre*, for he actually represents a return from the world of tribal man of the old mythical justice of *lex talionis*, an eye for an eye, the archaic blood vendetta of tribal societies like the ancient Scandinavians or the Arabs. Thus, the type of mythical consciousness that his actions signify actually subverts and undercuts the rational consciousness of due process presupposed by the builders of the modern megalopolises.

There is, furthermore, one other important structural element in this episode: the image of Tarzan escaping through the window out onto the crumbling rooftops of a moonlit city at night, a scene which foreshadows the advent of the rooftop dwelling superhero and his frequent entrances and exits through windows. (There is further to be remarked the fact that the vision of Tarzan dressed in civilized clothing walking the streets of Paris, where he is known as "John Greystoke," is roughly an equivalent of Superman's Clark Kent persona, and shows us that

Tarzan's psyche is already riven by the fracture lines of the schizoid ego which later characterizes most superheroes).

Consumers

The world of hyperreality discussed so often by postmodern philosophers–Baudrillard in particular–is already heralded in the figure of the comic strip incarnation of Tarzan who, beginning in 1929, channel surfs his way from one historical epoch to the next. As the Sunday strips (these, unlike the dailies, were in color) begin in 1931, we find him dwelling amongst the Arabs of North Africa, but soon a back alley of the jungle leads him through a time warp into the age of the dinosaurs. Then, while fleeing this world, he stumbles upon a fossilized survival of ancient Egypt, which becomes his primary adversary for a number of episodes. When he is finished battling that civilization–and he does, indeed, battle the entire civilization (for he is against civilization as such)–he encounters some pirates who carry him onward into a facsimile of Turkish Islamic society, then into an African tribal society, a Viking society, and so on.

Thus, the Tarzan of the comic strips already prefigures Disneyland, in which all of history is seen as going on simultaneously in the present, like a movie studio where one can simply cross the lot from the Roman Empire and walk into Napoleon's invasion of Europe.[13] This is precisely the historyless world into which Western society as a whole has slipped: a transpolitical, ahistorical landscape of simulacra without meaning or value.

Tarzan as a character, furthermore–especially in the novels–inhabits an ahistorical world of pre-cultural anthropoid man locked into a seven million year struggle to build the physical body while surviving amongst dangerous animals in an age where time does not exist and nothing of cultural import or significance ever takes place. This archaic world, oddly enough, has become *our* world *now*, the world of real time video monitor screens and ersatz cities, a world which exists in a similar kind of unending sameness of limitless temporality. We live in a (worldless) society nowadays in which culture has ceased to evolve, history has stopped developing, and only technology is undergoing anything like what we would call an evolution, although it is an evolution which acts as a disintegrative and destabilizing force on highbrow culture as a whole.

Thus, the invention of the superhero is tantamount to the creation of a series of avatars of a senile, aphasic, amnesic society that wishes to have no connection to the past, fight no wars of historical significance (hence America's reluctance to enter both World Wars) and to build an endless horizontal landscape corrugated by shopping malls and striped by freeways beneath the dome of a neon sky. The superhero as created by Edgar Rice Burroughs is a nihilistic protagonist who wishes to be cut off from the past and the realm of discourse altogether. He wants only to exist like an animal for whom the world knows neither past nor future but only an endless eternal "now." Thus, Tarzan is the prototype for the apathetic American consumer who cares nothing for ideas and is obsessed with his body (endlessly overfeeding it and then, stung by remorse, exorcising it of its caloric demons). Tarzan, with his disdain of civilization and his desire to simply hide out in the jungle with his ape companions and to be left alone (in a zoological garden of plenty where there is never a shortage of groceries) untroubled by the pangs of history, conscience or remorse, essentially *is* the forerunner of the average American consumer of today.

Tarzan, in short, is Nietzsche's Last Man at the End of History who dreams of no world horizons anymore, but only wishes for safety, security and material comfort. He is the ape who has left behind the troubled horizontal world of the unprotected savannahs which produced the traumas of history–and the history-making overmen who built civilizations–and returned to the vertical world of the trees and the jungles which protected the apes of the great southern rain forests to the *west* of the Rift Valley, where they survive, untroubled by the physiological deformations of evolution, in the form of gorillas to this day.

We must never forget that the crucial thing about Tarzan is that he wishes to *go back* to the trees in the Garden of Eden from whence humanity was expelled once, so long ago.

Thus, the myth of Tarzan, once more, embodies contrarieties, for he is *both* the complacent American consumer at the end of history–who wishes to *stay out* of history, and so substitutes endless consumption for revolution–and yet also the nomadic man of tribal society who has come to break apart that very consumer paradise. This is one of the reasons why his myth is so enduring, and is so endlessly mulled over by popular culture which reanimates it in films, novels, cartoons and children's books every few years. Subliminally, the myth fascinates because it works on so many levels at once and activates numerous myth complexes in the psyche which are working at cross-purposes with each other. Tarzan is both a child of Darwinian evolution *and* Gnostic mythology; he is both apathetic consumer *and* tribal nomad who wishes to set civilization on fire.

It is precisely because of his deceptive simplicity and subliminal complexity that we cannot let him go, and most likely, *will* not let him go for some time to come.

He may still be there, haunting the ruins of our sunken cities and vine-choked billboards and collapsed tunnels, long after the drama of Western civilization has played itself out.

Zorro and the Birth of Los Angeles

0.

With the advent of Zorro in 1919, we are shifting now from the figure of Tarzan–image of the nomadic hunter of the Paleolithic for whom the Animal is essentially a horizontal and equal companion–to the figure of the horse-mounted caballero as defender of primordial Los Angeles, as yet still a pueblo existing at about the level of a Neolithic farming village. Here, the Animal has become domesticated and no longer exists on a plane of horizontal equivalence with the human being, but functions now, as it were, *beneath* him; hence, the hierarchical symbolism of the man riding the horse.

Los Angeles in the days of Zorro (the town was founded in 1781, although Zorro's exploits take place in the 1830s or thereabouts) is basically a farming community made up of ranchos which radiate out from a central, flat-roofed pueblo surrounding an open plaza lined with a church, a jail, the guardhouse and a public granary. The town had a self-sufficient economy, for what was grown in the fields was eaten in the haciendas. Cattle were raised for currency, and their hides were tanned and cured while their fat was rendered into tallow. Things like blankets, textiles and pottery were made, but as yet there were no real specialists, for these will not arrive until after the Mexican-American War (1846–48) with the coming of the Anglos who will bring with them "grocers and druggists, retail and commission merchants, painters, plumbers, carpenters, and masons, physicians and attorneys, bankers and realtors, manufacturers of brick, millers of flour, and distillers of wine."[14] The Mexican culture of pre-Anglo Los Angeles, on the other hand, was a society of generalists with extended families and self-supporting farms. There was as yet no merchant class to speak of. "Their self-sufficiency," as Robert Fogelson remarks, "inhibited opportunities for artisans, merchants, professionals, and manufacturers, and precluded urban growth in the pueblo."[15] Indeed, boats carrying cargo to Los Angeles did no business in the town at all but rather transformed their ships into shops.

With the appearance, then, of the first of Johnston McCulley's Zorro stories, "The Curse of Capistrano," in *All Story Magazine* in 1919, the superhero does an about face from Tarzan's (and Nemo's) attitude of hatred toward cities to one of defense of its basic values, although these values are as yet pre-urban agricultural ones. Raising children, romancing, dancing and serenading lovers, fiestas, music and ritual: this is the world of El Pueblo de Nuestra Senora La Reina de Los Angeles ("the Town of Our Lady, the Queen of the Angels") that Zorro is concerned with defending against oppression by its governing Mexican authorities. It is a world as archaic and ancient as the first flat-roofed villages that began to arise along the banks of the Upper Euphrates in Syria at sites like Mureybet in 9500 BC and in the Rift Valley of southern Palestine at Jericho. Mureybet, too, was a cattle-raising community of farmers who worshipped goddesses and the cult of vegetal abundance from the soil. The nomadic civilization of the man on horseback had not yet arrived, but at La Reina de Los Angeles, he is there, in the shadowy figure of

Zorro, and in him, we are witness to the earliest signs of the domestication of the superhero by the nascent city.

1.

According to Marc-Alain Ouaknin, in his book *Mysteries of the Alphabet*, the letter "Z" represents "a weapon, or two armies confronting each other, hence the recurring aspect of two parallel lines." Its derivative meanings, furthermore, are interesting: "War, conflict, confrontation, revolution, fracture, distance, change, movement, crossing, to cross, quit, to move away, interval, energization, to challenge, questioning inadequacy, the logic of contradiction."[16]

How fortuitous, then, that Zorro's very signature carries with it a tradition of symbolic associations that fit him as a character, for he is always confronting someone over crossed swords and questioning authority. There is something vaguely revolutionary about him, and if we were to situate him within the context of Revolutionary France, he would fight on the side of the people against the aristocracy rather than his prototype the Scarlet Pimpernel, who devoted himself to rescuing doomed aristocrats.

The numeric value of "Z", in Kabbalistic tradition, furthermore, is 7; hence, with Zorro we are moving into the realm of Time, of the seven days of the week and of seven year Saturn cycles. The timeless, ahistorical world of Tarzan and his australopithecines is crumbling and giving way to the metabolism of cultures and cities, of historical processes of becoming and unfolding.

But "Zorro" also sounds like "zero," the plenum and fullness that is prior to Time and which survives beyond it, for zero is the egg that is pregnant with creation and exists in an eternal state of equilibrium. Hence, like the dual personality of Don Diego de la Vega himself, even Zorro's name is rife with contradictions and tensions that suggest a fundamental fracture, a basic instability, corrupting and forever poisoning any sense of inner tranquility.

2.

Of course, the word "*zorro*" in Spanish means "fox," and foxes in ancient mythology are normally associated with the realm of the underworld (they are nocturnal), as are canines generally. Thus Zorro is a shade, a revenant, a dark avenging spirit from the realm of the dead and the Ancestors, who has come back to punish the corrupt and the wicked. There is something sinister about him as a figure, and he belongs to the "Varuna" side of the "Mitra–Varuna" dichotomy that Georges Dumezil wrote about in his book of the same name.[17] In Vedic myth, Mitra (which means "friend") is the god of contracts and oaths, a solar figure of light and law and luminosity, while Varuna was the dark and ancient god of the sea and the nighttime sky who punished transgressors by binding them with ropes and nets. Thus, in the basic Mitra–Varuna structure, the one figure represents the Law and harmonious accord while the other points toward death, darkness, brutality and punishment.

The cheerful Don Diego de la Vega, then, who is the daytime friend of Sergeant Gonzales, metamorphoses at night into a dark, punishing avenger who challenges the very same Sergeant Gonzales to a duel with swords.

Once again, evidence of a schism, a line of fracture running down through the middle of Don Diego's psyche, and in this case, a fracture suggestive of an almost cosmic bipolarity.

3.

Zorro is a being who redresses imbalances, and there is a fundamental juridical nature to him that is entirely alien to a figure like Tarzan. But this juridicality is not necessarily that which governs the laws of man and his institutions, for he represents a much larger and greater cosmic law of homeostasis which the Greeks knew as *lex talionis*, the law of cosmic retaliations. As first articulated by Anaximander: "Whence things have their origin, thence also their destruction happens, according to necessity, for they give to each other justice and recompense for their injustice in conformity with the ordinance of Time." Anaximander was simply translating into the mode of Greek philosophical discourse the ancient Egyptian mythical idea of the Judgment of the Dead with a pair of scales: if your heart weighs heavier than the feather of Ma'at, goddess of Truth, then you will be dispatched to a great, slobbering beast known as the Swallower, who will engulf you entirely, with no chance of survival into the Afterlife. Thus, dark deeds weigh down the soul while good deeds make it lighter. In the discourse of Anaximander, this personal soteriology is translated into a more cosmic language that almost approaches the dignity of science: thus, the cold of winter makes reparation for the injustice committed by the heat of the summer; human life itself is a transgression against the natural boundaries of the elements and will be paid for by death. It is a cosmic law of homeostasis which keeps things embedded in a universal flow.

Zorro, likewise, is thrown forth by cosmic powers manifesting themselves in the human world as a figure who redresses imbalances. If, in a Zorro tale, we discover a military man unjustly punishing an innocent friar by having him flogged, we can be sure that later on in the same narrative, we will see Zorro having that same man flogged in order to redress the cosmic balance. If Captain Ramon commits an injustice upon Lolita Pulido by ravishing her and attempting to steal a kiss, we find Zorro forcing him to apologize to her for that very same action, thus playing it back in reverse, as it were.

Tilted onto its side, the letter "Z" does resemble, more or less, a pair of scales.

4.

In McCulley's original novel, whenever Don Diego puts on the mask of Zorro, the mask is described as covering his entire face. McCulley tells us that he has to lift up the mask in order to kiss Lolita Pulido, and therefore we are to imagine the original Zorro as a man with no face. (It was Douglas Fairbanks, Sr. who, in his 1920 silent film *The Mark of Zorro* changed the mask so that it covered only his eyes, thereby leaving the lower half of the face uncovered, and this is typically how the image of Zorro comes down to us all the way to the Antonio Banderas movies of the 1990s).

But the image of a man who has defaced himself by erasing his own features with a plain black cloth is tantamount to an act of the highest depersonalization. The human face is the very seat of individuality, the most characteristically expressive part of the anatomy in which all of one's quirks and uniquenesses are most readily evident.

Thus, when the clumsy and inept Don Diego puts on the mask of Zorro, he disappears as a three dimensional personality and fades into the collective realm of the Ancestors. The mask at once transforms him from a living and breathing three dimensional being, *this* particular man *here* at *this* particular point in space, to a faceless, flattened, two dimensional image of an eternal mythical Avenger, *the* Avenger, in fact.

The number 7, interestingly enough, looks exactly like the letter Z, only with the bottom line removed. Hence, in putting on the mask, Don Diego moves from the realm of Time and history (signified by the number 7, which, as we have seen, Kabbalistic theory ascribes to the letter "Z") and into the realm of "Zorro," or that of the timeless atemporality of ancient myth.

5.

But that is not all. For to disappear into the ancient realm of the shadows, the realm of Plato's timeless Forms, is also simultaneously to leave the personal and the historical behind in order to enter into the collectivity of the human species as such. The human species can be thought of as a single gigantic individual multiplied throughout space and time. To put on the mask and enter the realm of the timeless is to leave the historical conditions of the species behind in order to reenact the primordial conditions of proto-events, the very proto-events which the myths record as having brought things into being *in illo tempore*: the First Death, the First Sexual Act, the First Tool, etc. Thus, when Zorro is brought forth and the human persona of Don Diego is dissolved, the timeless atemporal mythic arena of First Events is opened up, and every act of vengeance inflicted by Zorro becomes also simultaneously a reenactment of the primordial Act of Vengeance. Hence, the significance of his cutting the letter "Z" into the flesh of his antagonists: an echo of God's branding of Cain as the mark of the First Act of Vengeance which sent a man wandering over the dark earth, consigned to be forever homeless while the metamorphoses of history go across the earth without him.

6.

There exists a widespread Native American myth about a man who marries a female fox. The story goes that the man comes home each day to find his house cleaned and put into order, and one day he discovers the skin of a fox and decides to hide it so that the woman to whom it belongs cannot put it back on. He then marries the woman who, however, eventually finds the hidden fox skin, puts it on and then disappears over the hills, having returned to her original fox form. The point of the story seems to be that the normal form of the woman is that of the fox and that the fox's human transformation is a mere episode of escape from her essential being as a fox.

With regard to Zorro and Don Diego, then, we may ask a similar question: is Zorro the mask which Don Diego invents in order to escape from the banality of his humanness as Don Diego, or is it rather the case that it is Don Diego who is the mask that Zorro puts on in order to escape from the tedium of the realm of Eternal Sameness of the archetypes?

Assuming the latter instance, we are then entitled to think of Don Diego as an avatar of Zorro, analogous perhaps to the avatars of Vishnu, such as Rama or Krishna, who are given temporary historical missions to accomplish. In this case, it would be Zorro who is the real being and Don Diego the shadow. Don Diego, like Clark Kent, is the mask of fallibility which the deity Zorro puts on in order to experience life in the fallen world. Don Diego, then, is the image of the human being after the Fall, the broken and inept survivor of the catastrophe of Becoming who is interesting precisely because of the damage done to him.

The ice cold perfection of Zorro would be insufferable without Don Diego as his shadow and counterpart. When Don Diego attempts to woo his beloved Lolita Pulido with the embarrassing suggestion that he send his servant to serenade her at her window on his behalf, we are able to laugh because we identify with his fear and hesitation. When, in the Douglas Fairbanks silent film, we see him performing magic tricks before a bored Lolita who merely yawns at his performances, we are amused by his naivete and simplicity. We identify with him because Don Diego is just like the rest of us, whereas Zorro is as cold and remote as a statue.

In McCulley's original novel, then, Don Diego and Zorro are two completely opposed beings and it is precisely the tension generated by their contrast that powers the narrative. This is why the Antonio Banderas movies of the 1990s fail to capture the charm and point of the original stories because in them, the Zorro persona which Banderas puts on is essentially no different from his Diego persona. Zorros trips and falls, leaps onto his horse and misses, exactly as Don Diego would have done. Thus, the whole point of the original myth has been lost.

7.

And the point of that original myth was precisely Don Diego's schizophrenic nature, for in McCulley's novel, *The Mark of Zorro*, it is as though the two personae have no awareness whatsoever of each other's existence, exactly as is the case with schizophrenics. Don Diego is the best friend of the corrupt and boastful Sergeant Gonzales, but as Zorro, he is Gonzales's enemy and treats him with contempt. As Don Diego, he attempts to woo Lolita Pulido's hand in marriage, but he is incapable of evincing any sort of passion at all. He is cool and remote and unromantic. As Zorro, however, he takes her in his arms and kisses her fiercely and duels his enemies without so much as a misstep.

With the advent of Zorro, then (although this was already foreshadowed by Robert Louis Stevenson's Dr. Jekyll and Mr. Hyde) the old Freudian notion of the ego as a monolithic entity is done away with and instead we are presented with a more Deleuzian multiple self or, as I term it, the Hydraic Ego. For the modern human personality of the Electric Age is a being stricken with multiple egos which the Freudian notion of the single, stable personality cannot encompass. The superhero whose left hand does not know what his right hand is doing is *the* paradigmatic figure of the Electric Age.

From this angle, the superhero invites a certain comparison to the modern celebrity who generates so many different versions of him or herself that they become confused, like Elvis Presley or Marilyn Monroe, about their very own existence. The superhero and the celebrity are enlarged (and exemplary) images—elongated to absurd proportions by the funhouse mirror of the mediatic Eye—of the modern psyche: we are *all* multiple egos nowadays and we must be such in order to survive the pressures exerted upon us by life lived at the speed of light. If, as Marshall McLuhan said, one response to information overload is pattern recognition through myth formation, then another response is schizophrenic crack up, for we must invent multiple personae to deal with different situations into which we are thrust as we are accelerated at light speed around the planet. Every electronic avatar in the ether that we generate is another *one* of "us," another mask of the hydra-headed multiple self.

Thus, the dawning of the schizoid superhero beginning with Zorro–and heralded by earlier figures like Jekyll and Hyde or the Scarlet Pimpernel–is tantamount to the erosion of the model of the self as discovered by Descartes in his *Meditations* or by Cervantes in *Don Quixote* at the turn of the seventeenth century. The superhero is to that older perspectival, Gutenbergian self what non-Euclidean geometries and aperspectival Modernist art is to the art of the Renaissance and Baroque, with its single fixed point of view and linear sightlines. In the age of multiple spaces and multiple times, the self, too, is composed of multiple selves.[18]

8.

Zorro is an incarnation of the collective will of the peasants of La Reina de Los Angeles. Thus, when Captain Ramon or Sergeant Gonzales are engaged in combat with him, they are not fighting a single individual but rather *the entire village of Los Angeles which has taken on form as a single man.* If Don Diego is an avatar of Zorro, then Zorro may be imagined as an avatar of Los Angeles itself, a shadowy representation of the collective will of the peasants who regard themselves as having been mistreated by the Mexican authorities.

9.

Although Zorro represents the hero in his ancient modality as the defender of the city, it is important to understand that he is nonetheless against urbanism as such, for his values as an avatar of the city are entirely those of an agrarian village. His main desire is to marry Lolilta Pulido and beget a family upon her and maintain the perennial village stasis of begetting the generations, tilling the soil and riding his horse. The injustices and brutalities which the authorities inflict upon the peasants and which Zorro sees himself as sworn to fight against are the result mainly of a series of transformations forcing the village out of its Neoltihic container and into the realm of modern city life. The shift away from Spanish rule in 1822 toward Mexican rule brought a number of destabilizing forces along with it, such as a rapid turnover of governors and an increase in criminality, while the Mexican–American War that came along in 1848 had the eventual result of ending Alta California forever. Rapid change, as in the case of post Cold War Russia, normally produces breeding grounds for crime and corruption, and it is this overarching metaphysic of the transformation of the pueblo of La Reina de Los Angeles into the urban metropolis of Los Angeles that Zorro's whole existence is dedicated *against*.

Unlike the towns and villages of the Late Neolithic, or the early European cities of the Medieval period, La Reina de Los Angeles was not constructed as a walled fortress (like Dutch New York) but rather as an open system integrated into a larger political assemblage which included a vast network of presidios, missions and other towns that were ruled from afar, from across the Atlantic ocean by Spain, and then later by Mexico. Hence, in the absence of these walls to protect it against the depredations of bandidos and corrupt military officials, the city grew for itself–that is to say, projected itself into three dimensional space–in the form of Zorro. In him we can see not only the earliest stirrings of the domestication of the superhero by the city, but also the relationship between the conception of the city without walls and the necessity for an internal immune system that will function as a way of maintaining that city's own sense of self-identity against disruption by noise in the form of crime and banditry.

Zorro is Mexican civilization's last stand against modernity. As a horse-mounted caballero he presides ironically over the very village that will later become the world's archetypal city of the automobile. The increase in speed from the nomadic hunter on foot to the horse-mounted rider has the result of obsolescing the way of life of the hunter, just as with the coming of the automobile, the man on horseback who had built civilization for four thousand years fades off into the horizon.

Of course, he will be retrieved in an entire genre of literature, the Western, of which Zorro is but one example. Hence, McLuhan's old adage that while moving forward, civilization looks backward through the rearview mirror.

10.

Consider the respective lines of flight of Zorro and Tarzan.

Tarzan's lines are erratic; they criss-cross and interweave one another as he moves nomadically back and forth across the jungle, and from the jungle to the city, or from one lost civilization to the next. He is like a comet which crashes into cities and long forgotten kingdoms as he collides with armies of hunters or soldiers. He cannot be contained; he appears suddenly from the trees above, effectuates an action, and then disappears just as abruptly. His movements, in short, can be modeled as a chaotic attractor.

Zorro's lines, by contrast, are not erratic, but circular. He orbits the pueblo of Los Angeles like some lost rogue moon caught in its pull. His hacienda is situated on the outskirts of the town, and he is constantly (and predictably) traveling between it and the town square. He never ventures far away from the town, for he is always hovering somewhere nearby. His actions would suggest the model of a periodic attractor.

Thus, with Zorro, the superhero becomes caught into the gravitational pull of the city and from henceforth, it will not let go of him. Here we see him falling, careening toward its center like the Gnostic Anthropos in the *Corpus Hermeticum* who has seen his reflection in the mirror of *Physis* and falls inevitably towards it. Soon, the city will trap him and he will not be able to extricate himself from it easily.

It will require the exertions of a Hulk to break free again.

11.

Zorro is like an acrobat: he is always jumping, leaping, flying through the air. Unlike Tarzan, he does not inhabit treetops, yet his feet are almost always off the ground. This is especially evident in the Douglas Fairbanks silent film, which shows him running, jumping from one balcony to the next, or leaping over a wall, swinging from chandeliers.

If Tarzan is born from the earth, then Zorro is always in the midst of trying to free himself from it. Isabel Allende in her 2005 novel *Zorro* plays with this idea by imagining the young Zorro temporarily joining up with a troupe of wandering Gypsies in Spain who put on circus shows beneath tents. He and his brother Bernardo perform an acrobatic act as they leap from trapezes.

In a way, Allende suggests a parallel between the superhero and the circus performer: both are endowed with a rich superfluity of ability which allows them to perform deeds otherwise impossible for the average man. However, there is a crucial difference: for the excess abilities of the circus performer are largely useless ones and have little or no practical value, whereas those of the superhero are purposive. Indeed, the circus is a cosmos set apart within the midst of a city in order to open a window into the world of miraculous abilities. But they are superfluous abilities: juggling plates; strong men lifting weights; flying through the air; swallowing fire; commanding the animals.

The abilities of the superhero, on the other hand, are teleological: when the Human Torch lights himself on fire, it is so that he can fly through the air and hurl fireballs at villains; Batman's mechanical ingenuity is an endless mine of gadgets that he uses to defend Gotham from the Joker's anarchy; Spider Man can walk on walls and crawl up buildings all the better to trap villains in his web.

Circus performers are cast off by the city like so much effluvia, for they essentially have no place within it, which is why they are always nomadic and live in the interstices *between* cities. Superheroes on the other hand...

Well, let's just say that the city has had its Eye on him all along.

12.

We have established, then, the presence of at least two worlds indicated by the schizoid identity of the superhero: without his mask, he exists in the realm of the personal and the individual, the three dimensional realm of the waking daylight ego. With his mask on, he shifts into the realm of the dead and the mythical horizon of the Ancestors, which is timeless and atemporal: an Eternity of shadows where demons are routinely encountered, like the snake-headed monsters and cat beings of the Egyptian afterlife.

In between these two worlds, however, there exists yet another, which is alluded to in the final pages of Allende's *Zorro*. At the climax of the book, Don Diego and his two companions, Bernardo and Isabel, all put on the identical mask and costume of Zorro simultaneously in order to foil their enemies. Thus, during the novel's conclusion, there is not just one but three Zorros.

With this image of the cloning of the superhero we enter into another realm, that of the metaphysics of capitalism, Seriality and Repetition, the realm of mass production and genetic cloning, of the indefinite repeat of Same over again. This realm, like the transpersonal, is also hostile to the three dimensional personality, but the transpersonal realm is made up of what Gilles Deleuze refers to as "individual singularities." That is to say, the figure of Zorro is unique and cannot be replicated, else he loses his authentic singularity, that which makes him essentially non-repeatable. He is transpersonal in that he is a timeless mythic archetype who has swallowed up the merely temporal personality of Don Diego de la Vega, but he is also fundamentally singular.

Through the act of cloning and repetition, however, the superhero is in danger of erosion, for he begins to lose his singularity as he degrades into the realm of the banal and the repeatable. This is the soupcan world of Andy Warhol's paintings; in fact, it is the nature of the metaphysics of capitalism, which mass produces singular objects and in the process robs them of their irreplaceability. They are at once transformed into the merely banal and commonplace. If Coca-Cola signs are everywhere, it is because there is nothing singular and unique about Coke, for it is instantly produced at the touch of a button.

Part of the very *raison d'etre* of the superhero's existence is a response to the capitalist realm of consumer clones and mass repetition of manufactured objects. The superhero himself is tantamount to a singularity, an Event, a discontinuity in the flow of capitalist banality. Once he is mass produced, he begins to dissolve back into the very matrix of Sameness which his existence is predicated against.

Hence, Allende's warning at the conclusion of her Zorro novel: the serial overproduction of the superhero will result in the cessation of his existence altogether. Through advertising, movies, cereal boxes, fast food merchandising, the presence of the superhero is being transformed via the capitalist machine into an ever present and ubiquitous icon, like Coke. He is descending into the realm of overproduction and mass cloning, for the capitalist machine is taking him over and the inevitable outcome is that he will lose the battle against the very Megamachine whose existence he is an objection to.

Thus, from McCulley's and Douglas Fairbanks's early Zorros to those of Antonio Banderas and Isabel Allende, we can see that the "individual singularity" represented by Zorro is on the verge of disappearing, for the myth is losing its original significance and may one day just fade off into the invisibility of the merely banal.

The Maltese Falcon
& the Cosmology of San Francisco

The Birth of Noir

Every noir narrative begins with a corpse, and in the opening pages of Dashiell Hammett's novel *The Maltese Falcon*—which was serialized in the pulp fiction magazine *Black Mask* beginning in September of 1929—we are confronted with the dead body of one "Miles Archer," a man whom, we soon discover, was the partner of Sam Spade. Together, the pair ran a private detective agency in San Francisco, and as the narrative opens, they are retained by one Brigid O'Shaugnessy to investigate a man named Thursby. Brigid had come to Spade's office under the ruse that she was afraid her seventeen year old sister had run off with this Thursby and was anxious that Spade and Archer investigate. By the novel's conclusion, we learn that Brigid had approached Archer in a dark alley and murdered him with Thursby's gun, a British-made Webley revolver, in an attempt to frame Thursby for the murder. It turns out that she had wanted Thursby, who had been her business partner, out of the way, for both she and Thursby had been hired by a man named Gutman to obtain a golden falcon made by the Knights of Malta and given to Charles

V of Spain as a gift during the seventeenth century. The falcon had made its way to Constantinople, where Brigid and Thursby had obtained it and then, instead of giving it to Gutman, had fled with it to Hong Kong, from whence, as the novel opens, it is on its way, by boat, to San Francisco.

Thus, like the Ark of the Covenant in *Raiders of the Lost Ark*, the black falcon is the central object of desire in Hammett's narrative, while Brigid is the central manipulator who has the male characters dangling on strings all about her. True to her namesake, Brigid is very much like a Celtic warrior heroine, comparable perhaps to Maeve in her ability to get men to do her bidding.

However, beneath the entertaining surface structures of Hammett's narrative–which is as smooth and streamlined as a fifties rocket-finned Chrysler–there lie some very interesting, and very ancient, deep structures organizing the narrative, structures which, when excavated, uncover the very bones of the noir narrative itself which here, with Hammett's novel, achieves its first true masterpiece.

Of course, *The Maltese Falcon*, published in 1929, was not the first detective story. It is a truism that Poe invented the detective genre with his three Dupin stories, which Wilkie Collins in the 1860s with *The Woman in White* and *The Moonstone* surpassed, and then Arthur Conan Doyle perfected with his famous Sherlock Holmes stories. But pipe-smoking Holmes, polite, suave and sophisticated, belonged to respectable society whereas Sam Spade–and before him, Hammett's earlier alter ego, the Continental Op–is a man of the streets, as callused and rough-hewn as most of the denizens of the criminal underworld that he hunts. Spade is something new and represents the birth of the noir novel, for he is the prototype of every hard boiled detective which came after him, from Chandler's Philip Marlowe in Los Angeles to Robert B. Parker's Spenser. Unlike most of those other narratives, however, *The Maltese Falcon* is a true literary masterpiece, for its plot is perfectly formulated and its prose is lean and spare. Moreover, the mythic structures of *The Maltese Falcon* show us how the noir genre operates as a mythology of the modern megalopolis all its own, giving us a sort of West Coast parallel to the contemporary New York creation of the superhero.

Names

First, let's consider the names (for names, when they are well chosen by their authors, can often act as excellent points of departure for the literary archaeologist to proceed upon his excavations): "Miles Archer" and "Sam Spade." Together they had formed a pair, running a private detective agency. Now, a spade is a tool used for digging into the earth, whereas an archer fires his arrows normally into the air, and sometimes–as in the case of ancient sieges–directly into the sky. Thus, the names would seem to indicate a sort of heaven-earth dichotomy. Miles Archer, as we eventually discover, happens to have been murdered by Brigid O'Shaugnessy, whose first name is the same as that of an old Celtic fertility goddess, patroness of healing, poetry and the smithy. Her last name is also significant, for it is the same as that of Michael O'Shaugnessy, one of the founding engineers of the city of San Francisco. Michael O'Shaugnessy built and designed the Hetch Hetchy aqueduct over controversy with environmentalists like John Muir, who resisted the industrializing of Hetch Hetchy, insisting that the beauty of the place deserved it to rank with the likes of Yosemite, and therefore ought to be left alone. Indeed, San Francisco (by contrast, say, with New York) was built out of a conflict between industrialists and environmentalists, and so Brigid's last name is a clue that she may have something to do with the fate of the city.

The Celtic goddess Brigid herself was a fertility goddess, and as such, was involved with the world of the farmer, who had to know her rhythms very well, indeed, in order to make a living from her bounty. However, in the history of the rise of San Francisco, farmers were the ones who lost out on behalf of the miners and engineers whose dams, aqueducts, timber mills and mines ruined his topsoils, robbed his water, and silted up his rivers. The run-off from mining projects like that of the Comstock Lode in Carson City, in which huge high pressure hoses (called "monitors") were used to wash away minerals from the sides of cliffs in order to reveal the treasures which they contained, caused particularly severe damage to farmer ecology by washing silt up rivers and making their water unusable for irrigation. In fact, the devastation wrought by industrial mining operations in the Central Valley between 1849 and 1884 was enormous: over 40,000 acres of farmland and orchards had been ruined and an additional 270,000 acres were severely damaged.[19] Huge tunnels were torn into the earth in order to dump afflatus into rivers like the Yuba. The waters of the Sacramento became so muddy that by 1852, salmon could no longer run in them. The course of hitherto placid rivers became subject to flash flooding. Debris was washed down into narrow canyons from mines, where it piled up. In addition, the raising of entire rivers out of their beds with the use of flumes required an enormous amount of lumber, deforesting huge swaths of earth in the process.

In 1878, farmers and townsfolk were forced to form an Anti-Debris Society in order to counter the Hydraulic Miners' Association. In 1884, Judge Lorenzo Sawyer issued a permanent injunction against any further dumping by the North Bloomfield Mining Company. But then the Army Corps of Engineers, with the stated aim of making the Central Valley safe for farmers, simply finished off the process of devastation, for "they transformed large stretches of its rivers into sterile ditches, annihilating whatever native plants and animals had managed to survive the initial onslaught of mechanical exploitation. Engineers successfully transformed California's Great Central Valley into one of the most intensively managed and artificial landscapes in the world."[20]

Indeed, the skyscrapers of San Francisco which line Market Street and created a concrete canyon out of Montgomery Street to the north (Montgomery and Market cross at right angles) were built and paid for out of fortunes made by these very same mining operations. The plundering of the earth and the desire to escape from it into high rises is tantamount to a proclamation of war upon the environment and all that lives in it, from farmers and ranchers to animals and plants, and so, upon the larger organism of Gaia herself. Even the cable cars which are such an icon of San Francisco today were themselves made possible by developments in the technology of mining, for the system of cables which they depend upon were invented by Andrew Hallidie, who in 1857 founded the California Wire Rope and Cable Company in which he used wire rope to carry ore skips across canyons on aerial tramways. In the 1860s, he and engineer Benjamin Brooks transformed this system into one in which passenger cars were pulled by an endless ropeway running in a slot beneath the street. The cable cars made it possible for pedestrians to access San Francisco's hilltops more easily, thus opening up a new real estate market on these previously inaccessible areas.[21]

Although this passage may seem like a street that leads us nowhere, in fact, by paying close attention to the graffiti on the walls of this street, we can begin to build a context of associations in which Brigid O'Shaugnessy's murder of Miles Archer can be understood as tracings embedded within a larger pattern. For Miles Archer, as his name suggests, embodies the heavenly aspect of the pair that he forms with Sam Spade, and so he points toward the skyscraping tendency of the city founders which, in Hammett's narrative, is caught, checked and overthrown by the old rustic goddess of the earth herself in disguise as a femme fatale. And Sam Spade, the digger into the earth—as well as into the lives of his clients—is essentially linked with the sphere of the mining magnate whose various metallurgical operations made his partner's ascension to the heavens possible.

Thus, Hammett's private detective heroes, from the Continental Op to Sam Spade, make up the immune system of San Francisco itself, for their values are precisely those of the city's: nomadic, rootless, misogynistic; lonely bachelors whose very existence is a refutation of the old agrarian institution of marriage itself. It is Spade's job (mythologically speaking) to identify those underworld criminals whose values are at odds with the city's and to return them back to Hades where they belong.

As in the Greek myth recounted by Hesiod, in which the angry Gaia sends her brood of Titans and Giants to war against the heaven-dwelling god Zeus—comfortably ensconced in his skyscraping residence atop Mount Olympus—so in Hammett's novel, the goddess brings along with her denizens from the underworld, denizens who are eager to capture Zeus's eagle. Gutman, for instance, the kingpin who has hired Thursby and Brigid to find the falcon for him, is essentially the chthonic serpent in disguise (a snake, remember, is merely a traveling "gut"). He weighs over 300 lbs. and visually resembles Jabba the Hut (in John Huston's 1941 celluloid version), although with respect to his function in the story, he is morphologically homologous to Fafnir in Wagner's *Ring* cycle, the giant who takes the gold as payment from the gods for building Valhalla, but is corrupted by its sinister power and turned into a greedy dragon. If the falcon, then, is the heavenly principle, Gutman is the resentful serpent who, like the nagas of Indian mythology, are forever cursing their antagonist, the solar bird Garuda. Gutman and his band of criminals are the dispossessed heroes of the underworld who, in an uneasy alliance with the offended goddess, wish to have their gold back, like Alberich in *Der Ring des Nibelungen* who wishes to take back the gold that was stolen from him but which he in turn took from the Rhinemaidens.

Where is this underworld located that Spade is attempting to return these criminals to? On a map of San Francisco, this turns out to be the underworld that is located to the southeast of Market Street, the old industrial and factory areas of the working classes where crime and poverty are part of daily life. Hammett's noir heroes try to keep the criminal incursions into the upperworld north of Market Street at a minimum, for north of Market, and along the spinal axis of Montgomery leading clear down to North Beach, lies the business district where most of his narratives take place. It is a fitting coincidence, then, that the North is traditionally the direction of the mythological upper classes: the abode of Zeus upon Mount Olympus, or Mt. Meru in the Himalayas; whereas the South, as in Vedic myth, is normally the direction of the underworld and of ghosts and spirits, as in the case of Crete vis a vis the Greek mainland (over which King Minos ruled as Lord of the Dead); or in *The Ramayana*, Sri Lanka, the island to which Sita is abducted by the evil demon Ravana; or in the Mesopotamian Gulf, the land of Dilmun which, identified with the island of Bahrein, seems to have been a necropolis to which the northern dead sojourned and over which Utnapishtim, in the *Gilgamesh Epic*, was given jurisdiction.

Thus, the private detective hero created by Dashiell Hammett in San Francisco is a sort of West Coast equivalent to the comic book superhero of New York City which, as I have shown in a previous book, emerged as a kind of immune cell to keep that city free of monsters and demons. But there is a crucial difference between these two types of heroes.

The Noir Hero vs. the Superhero

New York was the center of the radio industry, and as I have pointed out in *Celluloid Heroes & Mechanical Dragons*,[22] the effects of radio essentially brought the comic book superhero into being as an oral tribal warrior who solves problems in exactly the same way that they are solved in primary oral epics like the *Iliad* and the *Kalevala*, namely, through physical deeds of grand violence. A flip through the glossy pages of any Frank Miller graphic novel will confirm that they are blood-soaked throughout.

But the noir detective is different from the comic book superhero in that he does not triumph over his villains through physical violence—although on occasion he does resort to this—but rather triumphs over his antagonists by means of *ratiocination*. (Note that the hero of Hammett's novel *The Glass Key*, Ned Beaumont, who is smarter than everyone else around him, triumphs over his adversaries not with violence, at which he is inept, but by constantly outwitting everyone. He is the clever, wily, mercurial Odyssean type of hero which is the archetype of the noir detective.) The noir hero is essentially an *intellectual* problem-solver, for like Oedipus, he slays dragons through the power of the word rather than the sword. And, like Oedipus, he is normally presented with a riddle which he must solve, normally the inexplicable presence of a corpse which someone hires him to explain. Through the application of his mercurial intellect, he must go backward in time and reconstruct the sequence of causes that led up to the effect embodied by the corpse. Thus, he gathers up the component pieces like the separate frames of a strip of celluloid, and by the narrative's conclusion, projects them forth into a running narrative. The solutions are linear structures produced by the power of sequential thinking, the same kind of thinking that went into the analysis of physical motion through space via analytical geometry. The hero solves his crimes through the application of logic and reason, exactly duplicating the manner in which the scientist arrives at *his* conclusions by testing a hypothesis. The private detective is thus a vestigial survival into the popular, low resolution medium of the mystery novel of the very kinds of linear thinking which that medium helped to obsolesce.

Hammett's San Francisco, however, was not a newly literate polis, but rather a new city built within a culture in which the values of literacy were beginning to be eroded by popular narratives like the very ones in which the literate values of the noir detective were celebrated. This is perhaps why the noir narrative disintegrated as the twentieth century unspooled, and the values of popular culture, with its image worship and its mythological icon-based revival triumphed over the values of the Gutenbergian world of literacy. By the 1960s noir–at least in film–was a dead genre, while that of the comic book superhero, invented at about the same time during the 1930s, was just getting warmed up. For the superhero has nothing to do with literacy, and in proportion to the decline of literacy, he has become more and more popular, while the noir hero has been relegated to the rubbish heap of nostalgia for old black and white reruns watched by granddad–with his pre-television era attention span–in the back room.

Every noir narrative, as I have said, begins with a corpse. Then it moves backward through an analysis of the causes that brought this particular effect–i.e. death–into being. The image of a corpse laid out on a slab for deposition is where the Christian mythos *ends*, but this very same image is merely the beginning of the noir narrative. Thus Arnold Bocklin's painting *Mary Magdalene Mourning Over the Body of Christ*, painted in 1867 at about the same time as Wilkie Collins was writing the first detective novels, is the annunciation for the coming of the detective genre. Thus, as in the case of Western science, which emerged largely out of the study of dead bodies, it is a corpse which becomes the inspiration for the activation of analytical thought. And just as all higher thought originated with the problem of death, with the apprehension of the *thereness* of a corpse, so too, the linear thought structures of the noir narrative begin to march forth from a meditation upon death. There is, thus, a secret inward relation between death and literacy.

A corpse is something that is wholly space and no longer has any relation to time. The written word, likewise, in being divorced from the context of its evanescent uttering, no longer flows through time, but is something that *has become*. Words on a page, that is to say, only occupy physical space until they are animated–that is, put through the temporal flow–by the application of human thought. The Egyptians seem to have been the first to understand this, for the earliest origins of writing in Egypt come from tombs. The Egyptian god of writing, Thoth, furthermore, (whose name, perhaps, prefigures the word "thought") was *the* primary god of the dead, and was responsible for guiding souls to the underworld.

Without writing, and especially without *printed* writing, linear thought would not exist, for in pre-literate cultures thought is never analytical but something totalistic, for it exists in an acoustically resonant cavern space from which images bounce back and forth like sonic echoes, but within which they exist as separate and disconnected *things*, like an animal on the wall of a Paleolithic cave occupying its own private space and having no relation to the other animals as a whole. Cartesian phase space, on the other hand, is an intensely *visual* space, created by a linear, print-based mentality which is accustomed to scanning words from left to right on a printed page. It just so happens that this kind of linear process is the same kind of thinking that goes into the building of complex machinery, for machines must be carefully assembled step by step, not all at once. *Sequence* is of the essence of both machinery and literacy.

So, in the detective genre, there is a distant echo of all of this in the association between the analysis of the corpse as effect, as a sort of text, in other words, and the noir detective as a sort of scholar (or scientist) investigating how this particular text came to be written. The point being, here, that the noir detective is an embodiment of the values of the literate, urban and highly mechanized city, such values being the very opposite, not only of those of the post-literate secondary orality of electronic society, but also of those of the female, the right brain, the image, context, environment and embeddedness of every kind. Hence, Leonard Shlain's insight in *The Alphabet vs. the Goddess* that the revival of the goddess is connected with the decline of literacy is absolutely correct.[23] And correct, also, then, was Sam Spade's intuition that the woman named Brigid standing before him was a threat to his whole way of life.

Thus, the narrative of *The Maltese Falcon* is an assertion of the values of the city over against those of the countryside–as well as of hearth and domesticity–just as Zeus, in Greek myth, represents the values of urban, rational–and literate–Athens, against the ancient Pelasgian and Boeotian earth cults of the farmers. Athena, the official patron of the city, presides over the case of the matricidal Orestes in Aeschylus, and it is with Orestes that she sides against the ancient, bloodthirsty matriarchal Furies of Mother Right and the older, more chthonic Justice of the rural countryside. These very same structures are reiterated time and again in the archetypal noir narrative, in which the hero triumphs over a femme fatale. (James M. Cain's 1941 novel

Mildred Pierce, on the other hand, is the direct antithesis of *The Maltese Falcon*, for it celebrates precisely the values which that novel rejects: the independent woman, the suburbs, marriage, domesticity, children, etc.)

Indeed, in any given Hammett novel or short story, we can almost always be certain that a *woman*, somehow, somewhere, is to blame for the murder or murders with which his stories and novels begin. The woman in the short story entitled "The House on Turk Street," for instance, who manipulates three men into fighting for her and killing each other; or the character of Dinah Brand in Hammett's first novel *Red Harvest*, who is always in complicity with the novel's criminals; or the crazy women in *The Dain Curse* (Hammett's second published novel) Aaronia Haldorn and Alice Dain, who are guilty of murder and manipulation. Women, in Hammett's novels, are always at the root of the evils perpetrated, and they are in league with the criminals, because the criminals are the Titans, giants and monsters of his narratives, the underworld beings who are in alliance with Gaia, and who wish to overthrow the ruling city's power structures so that they can erect their own shadow economy of trade in crime. Notice that in Hammett's stories, his villains are always deformed somehow: the kid who barely talks above a whisper in *Red Harvest*; or the kid with a lisp in "The Whosis Kid"; or the deformed, inhuman ears of Gabrielle Dain in *The Dain Curse*; they always have limps, scars, stutters–like Walter Ivans in *The Glass Key*–and this not only marks them as physiognomically inferior and therefore criminal, but is in fact a distinguishing mythological trademark of underworld beings generally. In Irish mythology, for instance, the Fomorii who are the equivalent to the Titans of Greek myth, are all deformed: they have one eye, one leg or arm, or some other such monstrosity; and the same goes for the Titans of Greek myth and the *rakshasas* of Hindu myth. Underworld heroes tend towards physical deformity, for they embody the values of chaos in opposition to the harmony and orderliness of urban life in cities which, in clearing the trees and draining the swampy habitats of the countryside, make civilized life possible. Likewise, the transformation of the scarcely inhabitable desert peninsula upon which the city of San Francisco was built and made possible through the construction of aqueducts which brought life-revivifying water into the city, also erected a miniature cosmos by displacing and triumphing over a wilderness. The criminals in the underworlds of Hammett's novels are the very human equivalents of the chaotic wilderness displaced by the city and so they must be kept out of the city at all costs.

Thus, Brigid O'Shaugnessy kills Miles Archer because she is the equivalent of the bloodthirsty Furies who wish to exact vengeance on behalf of crimes against Mother Right. She is the dark chthonic cavern world of ancient night which was pierced and broken open by the rocket-like spires of Western European cathedrals and American skyscrapers. So the upward straining vector of modern urban society is deflected by her and thrown down. This countermove on behalf of the goddess against patriarchy is what sets the narrative of *The Maltese Falcon* in motion.

The Bird

The falcon is a bird that was, in ancient Egypt, associated with kingship. It was the symbol of the sun god Horus, the god which every living pharaoh incarnated, for the pharaoh had inherited his throne by way of Mother Right, since his claim to sovereignty was based on his genealogy through the female, not the male. In ancient Mesopotamia likewise, before the coming of the Babylonians, the paraphernalia of kingship–along with the right to rule–were bestowed on the king by a goddess, Inanna, who is depicted in numerous works of art bestowing upon him the rod and the ring of rulership. Inanna's bird, furthermore, was the dove, while Athena's was the owl, Aphrodite's the goose, and Brigid's the white swan. So, in the earlier traditions, birds were almost always sacred to goddesses, for as Robert Graves in *The White Goddess* has shown, it was later patriarchal divinities who came and took the bird iconography away from them, for Celtic Bran took his raven from the goddess Dana, as Odin took his two ravens from Freya, and as Apollo took *his* raven from Athena.[24]

The falcon in Hammett's narrative is then an ancient symbol of kingship and of the power of the goddess to confer it upon whomsoever she chose (recall that Hammett's falcon was made by the Knights of Malta, for the island of Malta was once, way back in the later Neolithic, one of the great strongholds of goddess iconography and religion). Originally, it would have been Brigid's right to bestow it upon whoever she chose to put upon the throne. In this case, her choice would seem to have been Sam Spade, but Spade will have none of that, just as the Babylonians rejected the theory of bestowal of kingship by the goddess and so changed the old Sumerian stories in which Gilgamesh was Inanna's paramour into an epic in which he specifically rejected her advances. As in the case of the death of Spade's sidekick Miles Archer, in the Gilgamesh narrative, likewise, we recall that it was the goddess who there caused the death of Enkidu when Inanna, after being spurned by Gilgamesh, asked the gods to strike his companion down with a mortal illness. We note, too, the similarity of the climactic confrontation between Sam Spade and Brigid O'Shaugnessy with Gilgamesh's clash with Inanna, for Spade, too, refuses to play the role of one of her sacrificial lovers. He says, "I won't play the sap for you," in reference to the deaths of the various men she has brought about, beginning with Miles

Archer on down to Captain Jacobi. He knows what fate such a role would require of him, just as Gilgamesh accused Inanna of the deaths and misfortunes of a whole litany of her lovers. Spade, likewise, will not be put on the throne as king of the city–for he mistrusts authority figures, anyway–but most certainly not by any mere woman, anymore than Gilgamesh, the Babylonian tribal hero, will agree to play the role of Inanna's paramour Dumuzi, whose fate is merely to die and be reborn through her womb.

So the struggle over the black falcon in Hammett's narrative is, on one level, a struggle for mythological rulership over the city of San Francisco. The golden bird which has fallen into a black enamel casing over the years is a fitting image of the staining of spiritual values by the coarsely motivated economic interests of the modern day. The criminals, Gutman, Wilmer and Joel Cairo want the bird because they believe it is worth money, and so their motives are purely avaricious, but from a mythological point of view, Gutman, as we have seen, is the serpent in disguise, and he actually wants revenge against his age-old nemesis the solar bird. Brigid, the old bird goddess in disguise as a femme fatale, wants the bird back because it is her rightful totem that has been taken away from her by patriarchal city builders. And Spade, the literate–and hence, anti-iconic–hero of the modern megalopolis, wants rid of *all* these mythic beings–birds, snakes, goddesses and all–for he is an extension of the immune system of the city of San Francisco itself.

The climax of the story, in which Spade reveals Brigid for the conniving murderess she really is, brings the narrative to its point, for Brigid is revealed from the misogynist's point of view as unworthy of possessing the right to rule the modern megalopolis, which is based on rational, literate values, and not upon the old mythological blood logic of *lex talionis*. She must be returned to her place in the underworld of Tartarus, and so in John Huston's film adaptation, the last shot, fittingly, shows Brigid being turned over to the authorities, placed in an elevator, and sent *downward*. She has been sent packing off to the underworld because the city must not be ruled by beings out of ancient myth, since such beings are right brain creations and belong to the realm of the image which the left brain, with its linear linguistic structures, has displaced. The goddess, with her entourage of dwarves and Jabba-the Hut style fat men, must be sent away by the civic hero as defender of the literate values of a rational polis.

Conan the Barbarian

Adorno for the Masses

Robert E. Howard's Conan the Barbarian is a floating signifier of the 1930s that can be plugged into absolutely any social formation or apparatus of capture whatsoever. The monthly pulp fiction format–for most of the stories were published in *Weird Tales* magazine–means that the hero must return again next month to fight yet another battle, and so Conan returns, relentlessly, month after month, to fight various monsters and villains, each story self-contained and disconnected from any of the others. Conan, then, as a barbarian loner from a northern kingdom known as Cimmeria, is plugged into a series of social formations: in one or two stories, he appears as a king, but in most of them he is some type of lone adventurer, pirate or mercenary for hire. The stories are formulaic and repetitious, as required by the demands of the pulp fiction medium: one Conan tale is just like any other. Hence, the same audience returns each month for another adventure which, like later television shows, guarantees them a fixed and unchanging set of signifiers.

In the 1933 Conan short story entitled "The Pool of the Black One," for instance, written by Howard and published in an issue of *Weird Tales* magazine, the story opens as a pirate ship named "the Wastrel" is abruptly boarded by Conan, who surfaces out of the waters as if from nowhere and immediately encounters a scantily-clad woman lounging around on the deck named Sancha (who perhaps resembles Princess Leia in *Return of the Jedi*, but what she would be doing on a ship full of lusty pirates is anyone's guess). After confronting the captain, who agrees that he could use an extra hand with the ship's duties, Conan becomes a temporary member of the crew, although they do not trust him and there is some friction between them.

After sailing for a time, the ship drops anchor near an island, and the men go ashore to explore it while the curious woman, Sancha, decides to swim after them and spy. Meanwhile, in a dispute on the island with the captain, Conan ends up killing him after he is insulted (he doesn't take insults well, this barbarian)–an act which the girl witnesses–and then happens to catch a glimpse of a tall figure darting past in the jungle carrying something on its back. Conan follows the figure to a strange and decaying stone city where, in an open courtyard he witnesses a secret ritual in which giant black men stand around a jade green pool while one of them plays a flute which causes their captive to do a strange dance. The captive is then seized by one of the blacks and then dipped upside down in the pool of stagnant green water. After the ritual is over and the blacks have filed away, Conan investigates and finds rows of shelves with small idols lining them, idols that can be held in the palm of the hand. He is surprised to see that one of the idols is that of the boy who had been dipped into the pool. He then notices the blacks moving once again through the courtyard, this time carrying the girl, Sancha. The black man holding her over his shoulders sets her down on the grass while Conan sneaks up behind him and runs him through with his sword. He and the girl then decide to flee, but the courtyard has four separate entrances and Conan does not remember which one leads out. Hearing sounds of the black men returning, Conan quickly replaces the statues that he had disturbed back onto their places on the shelves and then, out of curiosity, throws the body of the giant black man he had slain into the pool and watches as it shrinks and contracts into a small and calcined statue.

Then he and Sancha flee through the south gate, but the black men are returning, this time carrying all the crewmembers from the Wastrel who had obviously lain ashore eating something called the Black Lotus, which had narcotized them into trance states and rendered them easy prey. Conan hatches a plan to run through the western gate while the blacks follow him and to send Sancha back the other way to awaken the crewmembers. He proceeds to run through the archway which leads to an octagonal courtyard with no other exit and so, cornered, he fights the blacks. The sailors, meanwhile, once awakened by the girl, begin fighting the black men and flee for their lives, while the mysterious fluid of the green pool begins to rise up like lava into a single huge molten column that looms over them all. Everyone flees back toward the ship, while the phosphorescent green lava pours through the jungle after them like something out of an episode of the 1960s cartoon show *Johnny Quest*. Eventually, they make it back to the ship and leave the strange island behind them.

Howard, it should be noted, was notoriously poliphobic, for he regarded big cities as modern Babylons, and so the character of Conan, his most famous character, is a mask or an avatar worn by him for descending into an imaginary landscape in which Conan is always at odds with big cities and their political machinery. It is not too difficult to see, then, that in this story, "The Pool of the Black One," the bizarre ritual of the black men (aside from its evident racism) of dipping people into an insidious green pool that shrinks them down and turns them into statues becomes a metaphor for the culture industry–and is especially prophetic of the coming of television, that *blue* plasma pool–that has the effect of shrinking people down and turning them into idols and avatars, electronic ones, of course, but idols nonetheless (the television show *American Idol* would be a case in point). The green pool in the story is already pointing the way toward the coming of the electronic plasma pool that will soon, just after World War II, routinely transform three-dimensional–live flesh and blood–people into tiny electronic homunculi. Elvis Presley, for instance, as a domestic bodhisattva, or John F. Kennedy as a presidential golem composed out of electrons.

Conan's antipathy is *always* against the Big City, and the villains are *always* codes for the programmers and Big Men with Cigars who are in charge of the Culture Industry. Conan stories are Adorno for the masses.

Radio Days

Conan is, of course, like Gilgamesh or Beowulf, primarily a monster slayer. Indeed, the basic patterns are set up by Howard in the first few Conan stories. In "The Phoenix on the Sword," for instance–the very first Conan story, published in *Weird Tales* in 1932–we there find Conan in the atypical role of a king, namely of the kingdom of Aquilonia (barbarian France, in Howard's universe), a throne which he has usurped by murdering his predecessor. Four men are plotting to overthrow him: the leader of the conspirators, Ascalante, has a servant named Thoth-amon, who claims that he once had a magic ring in his possession and insists that one day soon he will find it again and use it to slay Ascalante. Sure enough, as he is talking with one of the conspirators, a man named Dion, the conspirator takes out that very magic ring–which is shaped like a serpent–which Thoth-amon recognizes at once and kills Dion to possess it (Tolkien, by the way, had not yet written his fantasy stories). Then he uses the ring to conjure forth a strange baboon-like demon with a mummy's face that he sends to go and kill Ascalante.

Conan, meanwhile, has been sleeping and having a strange dream about a long dead prophet who approaches him and marks his sword with the imago of a Phoenix bird. The prophet tells him that he will need it in order to fight Set, the great serpent monster. When he awakes, the four conspirators, together with their henchmen, have burst into the room to slay him and take back the throne. One by one, he kills them, but when the baboon-monster sent by Thoth-amon erupts into the room, he surprises everyone by going straight for the throat of Ascalante. After killing him, Conan then plunges his sword into the baboon-demon.

The story thus retrieves and sets up the archaic opposition machine of the bird / snake pair of signifiers: Conan has the Phoenix bird on his sword, while the ring that Thoth-amon used to send the baboon demon after Ascalante was in the shape of a serpent. The tale, then, is a simple one of the victory of the powers of the heavens against the earth-bound chthonic instincts. It is the old, old story of the neocortex and its evolutionary triumph over the reptilian brain. Conan is a type of the solar hero who presides over a universe of light that banishes the monsters and icons of the night with his sword: an evident extension of the rays of the sun.

A few stories later, however, in "The Tower of the Elephant" from 1933, Conan is not a king but a thief (he turns up in the role of king only very rarely, for Howard always wants him on the *outside* of the city-as-apparatus). In this story, he is told in a tavern by a boisterous man that the huge tower in the center of the city of Zamoria contains within it a rare and precious jewel named the Heart of the Elephant. Conan decides that he will steal the jewel and so sets forth toward the compound of the tower late at night. He meets another thief with exactly the same intention named Taurus, who agrees to aid him in his efforts. In the courtyard, they encounter a group of five lions which Taurus dispatches by blowing poison at them through a tube. They ascend the tower, but at the threshold Taurus is immediately killed by the sting of a giant spider which Conan must now combat. He throws a heavy jewel case at the spider, which kills it and then he enters a room where a man with an elephant's head is sitting upon a throne. His name is Yag-kosha and he informs Conan that a sorcerer has put a spell on him that has condemned him to sit in the tower forever. The evil magician, named Yara, also resides in the tower and the elephant-headed man tells Conan how to kill him: he must put Yag-kosha out of his misery and cut out his heart and then squeeze the blood onto the jewel known as the Heart of the Elephant, which he guards. Conan does as instructed and when he finds the evil magician Yara, he gives him the jewel as "the last gift from Yag-kosha." The jewel has the effect of shrinking Yara down to a tiny minuscule size and he disappears inside of it, held captive, presumably, for eternity. Conan flees as the tower begins to collapse into ruins behind him.

    On one level, it is immediately evident that with these stories Howard himself becomes a sort of tomb raider of the midden heap of the mythological age. The mythic epoch, which stretches from the first generation of civilization in the Near East down to about the time of Homer and Moses–when the beginnings of the mental consciousness structure, or Jaspers' Axial Age begins to take over–nowadays of course lies in ruins. It is composed of a slag heap of disused myths, broken signifiers, collected stories and fables compiled by the Alexandrian mythographers of today's age such as Carl Jung and Joseph Campbell. But Conan is a figure who raids this pile of signifiers, reversing their entropic waste into pop cultural metabolism. The elephant-headed man, for instance, is obviously the Hindu god Ganesha, and "Thothamon" from "The Phoenix on the Sword" is the god Thoth from Egyptian mythology, and so forth. Howard, like the Hollywood studios of the 1930s, is busy in these tales mixing and matching myths and metaphors from a broken-down slag heap which the metaphysical age–from Plato to Husserl–reduced to a pile of rubble. The myths no longer have any structuring planes of organization upon which to stratify them (no apparatuses of functioning capture, that is to say, such as mandalas or cathedrals), so their signifiers are now retrieved randomly by pop culture artists and put into play as intellectual action figures.

But on the other hand, the myths and gods of antiquity did not just die at the end of the nineteenth century with Holderlin's annunciation, in his poem "Bread and Wine," that the gods had departed from us moderns. The gods *have* continued, not so much in mainstream culture–where, during Modernism, one finds glints of them in the works of Joyce, Mann or Eliot–but in the Culture Industry of radio, cinema, pulp fiction and comic strips. The Culture Industry of the 1930s–in which radio was the dominant new medium–was a sort of negentropic machine for reanimating dead gods left over from the scrap heap of antiquity, and Howard's Conan stories are a glaring example of this sort of reverse entropy of a dead consciousness structure.

The villains in any given Conan story are almost invariably sorcerers, wizards and magicians: the men, that is to say, who preside over the phantoms and phantasms of the culture industry which Howard identified with the Big City. From this point of view, then, the tower in "The Tower of the Elephant" becomes an analogue for the famous RKO radio tower shown as the title card of many movies of the 1930s, beaming out emanations across vast distances, emanations which are caught and captured by radio receivers that then transform them into phantoms, monsters, giant serpents and men with elephant's heads. Indeed, the wizard in the tower–Yara–is a culture industry programmer, one of the Men Behind the Machine who meets a poetically just fate as the phantasmatic projector (the jewel itself) miniaturizes him and swallows him up inside of it.

Conan, then, is not just *any* ordinary old monster slayer, but specifically a slayer of the plague of fantasies (Zizek's term) which, during the 1930s, was projecting vampires, mummies, invisible men, serpents and giant apes onto movie screens and in through the labyrinth of the aural canal via the radio. Conan is erected precisely as a bulwark against what Freud dismissively termed "the black tide of occultism."

Indeed, as an example of these "radio days" in which the Conan stories are set, consider the tale "Xuthal of the Dusk," another Conan story published in *Weird Tales* in the autumn of 1933: in this story, Conan is wandering in the middle of a strange desert with a slave girl beside him, named Natala, whom he has rescued from one misfortune or another. They have run out of water and they see a distant city on the horizon that promises hope. Once through the gate and inside the city, however, they are confronted by an unlit realm of darkness and shadows where they encounter an effete man who seems to be in a trance and who assumes at first that Conan and the girl are not even real. But when Conan, at the point of his sword, convinces the man of his reality, the man explains that all the citizens of the city eat something called the Black Lotus and spend most of their time narcotized into a hypnotic dream state while a monster named Thog stalks the corridors of the city and occasionally gobbles someone up. Eventually, of course, Conan confronts the monster, kills it and escapes, with Natala, from the city.

The image of a darkened city full of spellbound people dreaming while awake is of course a transparent metaphor for the radio days of the 1930s, with people entranced in their living rooms or kitchens listening to the tales of The Shadow or The Green Hornet or some other such phantasm constructed by the Culture Industry. Robert E. Howard's Conan, then, isn't just a monster slayer, he is a signifier conjured up by Howard specifically to banish away the monsters and demons generated by the very same culture industry in which he himself was taking part through publishing his short stories in pulp fiction magazines.

It is no accident that most of the villains in any given Conan story are wizards, sorcerers or priests, since Howard associated such men with those in charge in the big cities who ran the machines–movie projectors, printing presses, radio apparatus–that sent forth the monsters and visions and dreams that collectivized and narcotized the American population into a trance, while the technician-priesthood surrounded and enslaved them with armies of machines while they weren't looking, such as Henry Ford with his automobiles. Howard, like Tolkien, was no friend of the cosmopolis, and preferred the rural countryside of his native Texas habitat.

Howard and Lovecraft

It is interesting to remark that Howard's correspondence with H.P. Lovecraft, which began around 1930, just before he invented the character of Conan, marked the beginnings of a friendship with just such a priest and sorcerer who specialized in calling forth monsters from out of the abyss. The friendship of Howard and Lovecraft continued until Howard's suicide in 1936, but Lovecraft was very much a real-life equivalent of the sort of priest of the cult of monsters that Howard always imagined his Conan avatar as battling *against*. Lovecraft, though, like

Howard, was no lover of Modernity, and though he invented perhaps the best and most imaginative monsters ever conjured forth on paper, he was equally poliphobic, preferring to spend his life in the quiet seclusion of Providence, Rhode Island.

Howard's universe, then, unlike Lovecraft's, is one governed by a hero descended from the Indo-Aryan dragon slayers of the mythical age, such as Indra, Thor or Beowulf. Like those heroes, he is a character who rejects the sort of astrologically deterministic universe conjured forth by Lovecraft (the monsters that Conan battles in "The Tower of the Elephant" constitute a veritable zodiac), in whose Cthulhu Mythos the gods and monsters of the pagan age return automatically when the stars align into specific configurations. Howard rejects such cosmic determinism, and his hero–one of many–is a disguised Texan cowboy who makes his own way in his own time; a loner who paves the way for Clint Eastwood Westerns and Mad Max movies.

It is perhaps surprising that the origins of swords and sorcery fantasy tales comes not from Tolkien but from an isolated American pulp fiction writer living in the Southwest, from out of whose imagination Conan emerged like one of the mind-born gods out of a Hindu myth.

With Conan the Barbarian, all monsters and gods from the mythical age are defeated, rejected and returned back to the slag heap from whence they came.

Howard specifically invented Conan to keep the smooth spaces of the Texan deserts free of such monstrosities as plagued the crumbling towns and rotting villages of the East Coast in the various stories of Lovecraft. Indeed, Lovecraft's tale "The Shadow Over Innsmouth"–in which the lone protagonist is besieged by an entire town of monstrous half-human half-fish people who chase him out–is precisely what results with a microcosm in which such a Conan figure is *lacking*. With Lovecraft, all mythological immune systems are breaking down, and indeed he himself died of cancer, a disease which—perhaps arguably—results from immune system compromise.

Howard's own life, on the other hand, ended with a bullet, in a fashion akin to a sort of modern act of *hara-kiri*, in which the disgraced sword-wielding samurai takes his own fate into his hands.

Conan, with his own sword, might have ended, one fine day, the very same way.

Third Media Transformation: Radio

The Shadow

The character of the Shadow was, in origin, a creation of radio. He debuted on July 31, 1930 as the host of the Street & Smith *Detective Story Hour*, and at first, he was only the narrator. But his persona was so interesting that he was immediately given his own pulp fiction magazine, entitled *The Shadow Magazine*, written originally by Walter B. Gibson and put out twice a month, beginning on April 1, 1931. However, the Shadow was turned back over to radio in September of 1937, where he was played by a young (22 year old) Orson Welles, who portrayed him for about a year until October of 1938.

As a character, the Shadow is almost totally displaced whenever he is removed from his radio environment, as the awkward 1994 film reveals. The key to his effectiveness is precisely *that he must not be seen*. He is entirely an auditory signifier, identified by his characteristic laugh, and it is notable that when one listens to the Welles radio plays, he is never described. The listener only knows what he looks like because of the spectacular cover images of his pulp fiction magazine, which depict him dressed in a black suit, black cape, black hat and a red scarf that covers his mouth. In the radio plays, the other characters only know he is there, because they can *hear* his voice, which Welles speaks as though through a primitive telephone. As Lamont Cranston, however, his voice sounds just like everyone else's. Thus, in a sense, the radio has gobbled up the telephone, for whenever the characters are speaking to him, it is as if they are talking on the phone.

The Shadow has learned various sorts of occult and magical abilities from his apprentice years with yogi masters in the Far East. They have taught him the ability to "cloud men's minds," as his tag phrase goes, which means that he can speak telepathically with them, often interrupting their thoughts. And when he is present, no one can ever actually see him. They only hear his voice as though it were coming from some dark corner of the room. He also has the ability to read thoughts and also to cause people to see things that aren't really there. His superpowers are, in this respect, rather unique and really only function within the context of acoustic space–which is spherical, since sound comes at us from a 360 radius–configured by the radio medium.

He is, in short, an avatar of what Jean Gebser called the "magical consciousness structure." This marks him as very different from most other superheroes, who are almost all reactivations of signifiers from the "mythical consciousness structure," which had its heyday with the first generation of the great civilizations in the Near East. The magical consciousness structure, on the other hand, is an aboriginal, tribal orientation to the world, in which magical resonances are sent out through it precisely because it is imagined as a single, gigantic point-like unity. In this respect, the world is almost like a sort of giant spider's web: when you touch one part of it, the whole thing vibrates. (Whereas, according to Gebser, the mythical structure begins to differentiate space and time as Heaven and Earth, with a macrocosmic soul–Brahman, let's say–and a microcosmic breath soul: the atman. Space is not so much spherical here as it is quadrated; and time is circular. In the mythical world, as Vilem Flusser remarks, everything always runs around in circles, until writing came along to cut those circles into lines with the alphabet, which originated as a criticism of myth with the Hebrew prophets and Plato. Hence, whereas the Shadow reactivates the magical structure, Superman, Batman, Spider Man and the others are mythical, while Sherlock Holmes or Sam Spade are heroes of the mental consciousness structure).

The cosmology of the magical consciousness structure is, as I have said, spaceless and timeless. Neither space nor time have been differentiated from out of it and since the world is conceived as a unity, spells can be cast which actually work through sending out resonances across this world-as-cavern.

Modes of communication, in this structure, are often telepathic. Recall the stories, for instance, of Westerners going to visit yogis in the Himalayas who "already knew they were coming." There is also a mouthless motif that exists within the imagery of this structure, in which the mouth–which Gebser associates with the mythical structure (for it tells stories and begins to open)–is closed and so communication is telepathic. Hence, the red scarf covering the Shadow's mouth.

Radio is an acoustic medium that, as a technology, reactivates the oral-tribal modalities of culture, or what Deleuze and Guattari call "the pre-signifying sign regime." A character who is precisely *non-visible* emerges from out of its electromagnetic Umwelt, a character who thrives on dealing with common criminals–gangsters, bank robbers, counterfeiters–specifically by interfering with their thinking. That is the Shadow's special ability: to disrupt thought like the voice of an angel from the ancient world, and to cause men to think *otherwise*. The ability, note, is magical in the sense that it depends on sending out thought *resonances*, unlike the usual superpowers of breaking things, sending out ice shields, creating webs or throwing hammers. All those are the attributes of the deities and heroes of ancient myth. Spell-casting and telepathy, on the other hand, are a vestigial survival from a much older, earlier stratum of consciousness that is perhaps as archaic as the Paleolithic.

One of the Orson Welles radio plays, "The Temple Bells of Neban," is a fine showcase of the Shadow's abilities. It was broadcast on October 24, 1937 and as the story opens up, Lamont Cranston and his girlfriend Margot Lane are out for a night on the town. They discuss how bad the situation has been lately with narcotics, but Cranston says he has no interest in being the Shadow for one night (Margot, unlike Lois Lane is fully aware of Cranston's dual identity). They go into a nightclub called the Club Caliph where they notice a young man known to them named Jerry Gleason who seems to be out of sorts. They meet a Hindu snake priestess who introduces herself to Cranston as Sadi Bel Abba, who makes a vaguely threatening comment implying that she knows his secret identity. However, she goes on with her act, after which, Margot and Lamont observe her talking for a moment with Jerry Gleason and take note of the connection.

In the dressing room after the show, we hear her talking with a man about a drug deal that will involve extorting a large amount of cash from a wealthy man. But the Shadow appears in the dressing room–or at least, his voice does–in which he warns Sadi to leave the Gleason boy alone, since she is obviously selling drugs to him. She points out that she knows who he is and that she is in possession of a power greater than his, namely, command over a spell known as the Temple Bells of Neban, a spell that has the rather unique property that when its final note is heard, it has the power to disintegrate Cranston's Shadow persona. She says she will see him again.

In the next scene, the city Commissioner receives a visit from Andrew Gleason, a very wealthy Wall Street banker who complains that his son is doing drugs and that it is the Commissioner's job to clean up the streets. The Commissioner then receives a phone call from the Shadow telling him more or less the same thing.

Lamont and Margot, meanwhile, hear three notes of the spell of the Temple Bells of Neban. He explains to her that he learned the power over the spell while being apprenticed to a yogi in India whose young niece used to listen in closely to their lessons. He suspects that Sadi bel Abba is the same girl, now grown up. He tells Margot he is going to the zoo to borrow a particular animal, but Margot hears a sound and when they look up they see a dead cobra hanging from the door with a note attached to it that reads: "Dead cobras are better playthings than live ones."

While he is drying out, Jerry Gleason hears the telepathized voice of Sadi in his head telling him to go to the dock and board a specific ship where he will find more drugs. Onboard ship, the Captain tells Sadi that the Gleason boy is now safe in the hold and that they will use him to obtain money from Andrew Gleason, his rich father. Then the Shadow's voice is heard challenging them, but Sadi says she will now use the spell of the Temple Bells of Neban on him. The Shadow warns her not to open her wicker basket to make the snake dance to the song, but when she does, the cobra leaps out and stings her death. The Shadow had replaced it with a cobra borrowed from the zoo. Thus, her spell is nullified, while the cops show up to clean up the scene.

Thus, the story is essentially a catalogue of the magical consciousness structure: telepathy, spell casting, magic, astral projection, etc. All its phenomena, moreover, are *acoustical* in nature, and therefore perfectly suited to the radio as a medium.

The ancient Egyptians called a person's shadow the *khaibit* and imagined that it could be detached from the body at death and live on its own after the body was mummified. With the Shadow, then, as a character, the new acoustic technology of radio—which tribalizes wherever it goes—reaches into the dim past of the Egyptian midden heap and reactivates from their long dead papyri a shadow entity known as the *khaibit* which now becomes tied to the city of New York as part of its slowly evolving immune system.

One by one, cell by cell, New York begins to construct an immune system to fight its crooks, swindlers, con men and thieves. The villains which the Shadow fights—at least in the radio plays—tended to remain common ordinary everyday criminals, unlike with Superman and Batman who tended to fight super-villains.

But the Shadow, as an acoustic signifier, is not *visual enough* for the New York pantheon, which will require men in colorful costumes to capture and dazzle the eye and imprint upon it an inner universe of American bodhisattvas and heroes. Radio, therefore, is not a particularly good medium for the superhero to flourish. For that, he will need comic books and splash panels, and then later movies and graphic novels.

Fourth Media Transformation:
The Comic Strip

Flash Gordon

Flash Gordon was a comic strip drawn and plotted by Alex Raymond beginning in January of 1934, and lasting until February of 1945. It appeared every Sunday, in color, for eleven years. It was originally conceived as a sort of knock-off of the Buck Rogers comic strip, which had begun in January of 1929 (at the same time as Hal Foster's Tarzan comic strip). These (along with Dick Tracy in 1931) were the first adventure heroes to appear in comics, which previously had been a medium concerned almost exclusively with "funnies" and social satire of the Krazy Kat and Little Nemo type. (In 1933, meanwhile, the first actual comic book had appeared in the form of Eastern Color's 36-page one shot publication of *Famous Funnies: A Carnival of Comics*).

Flash Gordon inhabits the world horizon that was opened up by Edgar Rice Burroughs with his John Carter novels, in which an earthman travels to another world where he becomes a superhero who rescues captured maidens from oppressive Bronze Age-type societies ruled by despots. Unlike the character of John Carter, however, Flash Gordon is not given any additional superpowers in the alternate reality that he inhabits. Such powers as he possesses simply derive from his nature as a blonde, athletic sporting type with exceptional fighting abilities.

But the key thing about Raymond's narrative is that it begins in the air. As the strip opens, Flash and his girlfriend Dale Arden are on a biplane that is hit by a meteor kicked up by the approach near Earth of a rogue planet known as Mongo. After safely parachuting to the ground, Dale and Flash are taken hostage by one Dr. Zarkov, who forces them at gunpoint into his rocket, which he has designed for the express purpose of crashing into the approaching world in order to deflect it from its collision course with Earth. But when they land on the planet of Mongo, the three discover that it is a world with its own civilization, tyrannized over by Ming the Merciless, who immediately captures Flash's girlfriend and tries to force her to marry him. Such plot as the narrative possesses is concerned with Flash's various attempts at rescuing Dale, pairing up with Zarkov (a technical genius who provides Flash with many escapes). Flash's sidekick for a time becomes Thun, the lion man, who aids him in fighting various monsters and dinosaurs who threaten the order of Mongo's civilization. And so forth.

Beginning with a relentless grid of twelve panels (which gradually compress and simplify over time to just a few iconic images), the overall impression which the narrative conveys–witness the name "Flash"–is one of speed: Flash is constantly on the move, jumping from one spaceship to the next, engaging in combat with one monster or oversized combatant after another; panel after panel depicts ships drilling into the earth's core or tumbling to the ocean's depths or racing through the skies from cities hanging suspended amongst the clouds; armies of hawkmen swooping down from the heavens, or chariots with dragons pulling them sweeping through clouds of dirt. Sword fights, ray gun battles and ships falling, crashing, blasting and zipping through the skies. One can see why it is often considered the prototype for George Lucas's *Star Wars* films, since Lucas lifted whole panels from the series (the cloud city of Bespin, for instance, is taken directly from the city of the hawkmen).

Indeed, it is no accident that *Flash Gordon* begins in the air and is characterized predominantly by movement, since by 1934, Western civilization was beginning its shift from one World Age to the next. As Peter Sloterdijk, in his book *In the World Interior of Capital* demonstrates,[25] air is the characteristic element of the third phase of globalization, a process which he envisions in his grand narrative as taking place in three distinct epochs: the first, beginning with the Greeks and their discovery of the rotundity of the earth and Aristotle's concomitant theory of etheric spheres in which the planet is situated at the center of all things and in which earth itself is the primary element; this is then followed by globalization phase two, beginning with the voyages of the Portuguese navigators in the fifteenth century, in which water becomes the primary element as ships of discovery traverse the earth's actual surface to reveal the astonishing extent, hitherto unknown, of the earth's submersion in the aquatic element. With globalization phase three, beginning around 1945, air becomes the primary element as airplanes, satellites and rockets displace the slow-moving sea-going ships of globalization phase two. The earth is surrounded with electromagnetic pulse signals that go racing from antennae across the surface of the ever-flattening globe, and soon, satellites are in orbit and rockets headed for the moon.

By 1934, Charles Lindbergh had already accomplished his famous transatlantic flight from New York to Paris in 1927; Hugo Eckener in his *Graf Zeppelin*, had circumnavigated the globe in 1929; and Wiley Post, in 1931, had accomplished the same feat in an airplane. Flash Gordon, as his name indicates, is the inceptual hero of the age of globalization phase three, in which rapidity of transport in, around, on, over and above the earth's surface becomes the prevailing characteristic.

The speed of the narrative, furthermore, is like the light particle in Einsteinian physics which, in approaching the speed of light, collapses into the singularity of two-dimensional space and infinite mass, for the narrative itself constitutes a flattening out of all traditional narratives into the degree zero of narrative continuity: not only are the characters dimensionless points, but the plotless narrative, heading for no goal and characterized by no development, represents the *absence of all narrative at the speed of light and its collapse into episodic momentarity*. As one turns the pages of the collected strips, the reader realizes that no actual story is being told or will ever unfold. Each week's group of panels *is* the point of the narrative: a momentary jam that Flash, as he accelerates across the globe of Mongo (a stand in for the earth itself) finds himself stuck in and must figure out how to disentangle himself in order that he may continue, like Deleuze's nomads, crossing the smooth spaces of the earth through the elimination of its striations which function as mere obstacles in the path of his conquests. Each episode of the comic strip, that is to say, represents the pure present, void of past or future, which the information revolution has gradually forced the planet's interior mind to collapse into: a dimensionless present in which the space of deferred time, a la Virilio, no longer exists.

Thus, Flash Gordon is a scaling down and miniaturizing of the ancient tribal oral epics–it is a "pocket epic" for the common man–with the crucial difference that it is actually no epic at all, but a pure narrative point with zero dimensions. Whereas the ancient tribal epics were two-dimensional and ran round in circles like the Eternal Return of the mythical consciousness structure, the Flash Gordon comic strip heralds the collapse of all narrative in the age of global electric simultaneity and speed-up.

It is a historyless world that globalization phase three has been constructing for us over the decades, and appropriately for Flash Gordon, the floating cities, transcendently self-contained and cut off from nature, which Flash continually encounters, are analogues of the City of Tomorrow that would be featured in the New York World's Fair of 1939, the very world's fair that would inspire Walt Disney to create Disneyland, in which the city of the world's fair becomes captured and miniaturized as Tomorrowland. This is the Crystal Palace of the Great Exhibition of 1851, which first announced the self-enclosed biodome of capitalism's world interior, a utopian ideal which the cult of technology and progress has striven to realize as the New Jerusalem on earth ever since. Flash Gordon becomes the immune cell of this City of Tomorrow and the various monsters and dragons that he fights are the threat constituted by nature and the environment that must be eliminated from its smooth-functioning at all costs so that the City of Tomorrow–Ming's metropolis–may be sealed off under the very glass dome which Disney imagined his EPCOT city in Florida would become: a historyless utopia cut off from flows of all kinds, the chronological flows of temporality itself, as well as the metabolic flows of nature, with all its rivers, air currents, entropy and weather systems which threaten to erode the stable fabric of this world city.

The city defended by Flash Gordon and lorded over by Ming the Merciless in 1934 would soon become, during World War II, the very ideal utopia which the Allied Powers would fight for–in opposition to Hitler's and Speer's reimagination of Berlin as Germania, a city embedded in Neoclassical fossilization–and actually seek to realize as the kingdom of God on earth, the very global aeropolis which we consumers today inhabit and take for granted.

Flash Gordon's battles against the various armies of Lizardmen, Hawkmen, yellow men, Sharkmen and so forth represent the resistance put up by the American utopia to the world's various historicalities and localities which it has sought to eliminate and dominate with the overcoding of its single anthropological type: the global consumer who, like ancient Mercury, with wings on his heels, is variously engaged in flying, shopping, swiping and spending. And soon, Amazon will be sending packages to his very doorstep with tiny remote controlled drones that will deliver packages to him by air in less than half an hour.

What else is this, but the world that Flash Gordon was already fighting for at the inception of globalization phase three in 1934?

Fifth Media Transformation:
The Comic Book

On Superman and Batman

Like the first mammal born as a singularity from out of the reptilian stream of evolution which anteceded it for millions of years, the comic book, too, emerged as a singularity, a *color* singularity, that is, which budded off from the Sunday funny strips in 1933. The Sunday funnies, in turn, had been contained within the black and white medium of the newspaper as a color anomaly for decades before they finally attained independence with the existence of the comic book, an all color medium that made possible a new environment that could be populated by new heroes. For the superhero, as we have seen, entered the comic book universe from without, essentially as a transplantation from the realm of pulp fiction periodicals, and so it is fitting that its first great superhero, Superman–whose debut appearance was in *Action Comics* #1 of 1938–is almost the only superhero ever to be imagined as arriving upon earth from another world. The story of Superman's descent from Krypton in a meteorite is actually a disguised narrative of the arrival of the adventure hero, who comes crashing into the universe of Sunday funnies previously inhabited exclusively by tricksters and funnymen like Krazy Kat or Little Nemo. It is also an image of the ancient Platonic myth of the soul's descent to earth from the cosmic architecture of the whirling spheres above.

Clark Kent, according to this semiotic, functions as the temporal, transitory human entity–a being constructed out of the four elements of earth and air, fire and water–that houses the soul as a spiritual being from another world. Once upon a time, this myth, as articulated by Plato and the Orphics who preceded him, was imagined as the ontological basis of *all* human existence, for every human being was regarded as a soul that had fallen from heaven to earth in a material body, but by the time of 1930s America, the scope of the myth had been restricted to that of an exception and a singularity. Only Superman *inside* of Clark Kent now is a being from another world. The rest of us are only material inhabitants of decaying world cities like Metropolis.

Of course, the colors of Superman's outfit–red, yellow and blue (a refreshing change from the Shadow's colorlessness)–are the Catholic colors once associated with the Medieval and Late Renaissance portraits of Mary and the Christ Child. The blue of her garments was meant to refer to the daytime sky, and the red in them to refer to the blood of Christ, while yellow was the Byzantine gold background of the magical efficacy of the Holy Spirit that moved and made itself effectual in the world through the deeds of saints and martyrs, beings, such as St. Christopher carrying the Christ child upon his back, capable of feats of immense strength and inhuman abilities. The birth of Christ was, according to Hegel, *the* Axial Event of history in which a single supreme being, the Son of God, incarnated in human form once and once only, but in the age of New York comic book cosmologies, the incarnation Event is recoded as an axial event of the world savior descending into this world from the Great Beyond bearing the signifiers once assigned exclusively to the Christian Savior: blue for the daytime sky, red for blood and yellow for the sun, the sacred day of rest in the Christian tradition that identified Christ's birth with the winter solstice and the advent of the New Light of Salvation.

Christ arrived as the World Savior—the fisher of Men—just as Superman arrives as a World Savior, initially designed by Siegel and Shuster, his Jewish creators, as an entity who would save humanity by extracting it from the tyranny of machines and their mad scientist creators. His early villains are accordingly, and almost without exception, mad scientists (the Ultra-Humanite, Lex Luthor) and big businessmen, and the plots of the first stories usually involve saving someone from victimization by technology and industry.

In *Action Comics* #38, for instance, ordinary people are committing robberies for no apparent reason. When a bank alarm is set off, Lois Lane and Sergeant Casey arrive to inspect the contents of its vault, but the bank manager closes the door on them and locks them inside, then resumes business. Superman arrives and destroys the vault's door, and the bank manager is arrested. Later, two bank messengers place their cargo in an armored car, but the driver fires at them and makes off with the money. Superman, hovering up above, is surprised to see Lois Lane show up and help the crooks toss the loot into her car. When he goes back to her apartment to investigate, Superman finds a clue to her strange and erratic behavior in the form of a mysterious black box hidden behind her headboard: a radio-controlled apparatus which he then finds in the houses of all the other citizens who have been committing crimes. When he follows their transmission signals to the radio tower from which they emanate, he finds a prominent psychologist broadcasting hypnotic instructions to these zombie-like individuals who are seduced into carrying out his wishes. The Frankfurt School theoreticians could hardly have done a better job excoriating the Culture Industry for corrupting the masses and transforming them into extensions of its will.

In *Action Comics* #12, to take another example, Superman goes on a rampage after a friend is killed by a reckless driver. He swoops down on a parking lot filled with the automobiles of traffic violators and proceeds to wreck every car in the lot, then picks up the car of a drunk driver and hurls it from a bridge, with the driver still inside. Then he goes to the automobile factory where, as the caption reads, "Gleefully, Superman runs amuck destroying the factory's manufacturing equipment." At the climax of the story in *Action Comics* #18, likewise, Superman destroys the printing press of a crooked newspaper publisher. "Into the great machinery," the text reads, "wades Superman, tearing the great steel monsters at terrific speed…"

The splash pages, furthermore, of the early issues of *Action Comics* all begin by taking delight in featuring Superman smashing up one or another machine or gadget: a streetcar (*Action Comics* #7); a tank (*Action Comics* #9); an airplane (*Action Comics* #10); a train (*Action Comics* #13) and so on. It isn't until *Action Comics* #20 (January, 1940) that a splash panel features him for the first time using his powers on *behalf* of the Megalopolis as he upholds a broken elevated train track just in time for the cars to get safely across.

Siegel and Shuster's avatar of the Being from Another World who has come to save us all, then, was specifically imagined as saving us all from science and technology.

This was not the case, though, with Batman, whose first appearance was in *Detective Comics* #27 in May of 1939, a creation of writer Bob Kane and artist Bill Finger. Beginning with the appearance of the Batgyro in *Detective Comics* #31, which resembles a small plane shaped like a bat with a helicopter rotor attached to it (and which was inspired by a drawing of Leonardo's), Batman's semiotics are more authentically Faustian, for he is a god of the machine par excellence (whereas there is something faintly Maccabean about Siegel and Shuster's hero who enjoys smashing the machinery of capitalism). Indeed, Batman is famous to this day for constantly inventing gadgets as supplements to his physical soma since that soma does not have any superpowers associated with it, and so Batman, like Western Civilization generally speaking, derives his power from technological supplements which extend and amplify his physical body: the Batplane, the Batmobile, the Bat-this, the Bat-that. If Superman begins as the being from another world who is hostile to the big city and takes delight in smashing it up (at least, in the early days), Batman is, right from the start, an immune cell who defends it from such vandalism: in *Batman* #1, for instance, when a horde of giants is going around smashing up el-trains and destroying cars (exactly as Superman is depicted doing in the splash panels on the first pages of the early *Action Comics*), Batman shoots them down with his state of the art Batplane, which comes complete with Gatlin guns. In the story's climax, he chases them to the top of the Empire State Building and showers them with bullets like an immune cell targeting a pathogen. It is the civilizational equivalent of phagocytosis.

Batman, of course, is a figure of the night, like his totem animal the bat, who derives his power from the moon, that symbol of time and ephemerality which governs the rising and falling of the towers and buildings erected by civilizations throughout history. His primary symbol, furthermore, is the cave, whereas Superman's is the mountain, from whence his Fortress of Solitude is erected (it was not originally at the North Pole, but on a sunny mountaintop). The cavern is linked with the underworld, for it is an ancient place for the burial of the dead that goes all the way back to 400,000 BC when the proto-Neanderthals of

Atapuerca, Spain were tossing their dead into caves. Superman, then, comes down from the sky; Batman comes up out of the earth. Their associated elements are in diametric contrast: sky vs. ground; air vs. earth; mountain as against cave.

(Marvel Comics, at about the same time, meanwhile, with their creation of the Human Torch and his battles against Prince Namor, the Sub-Mariner in *Marvel Comics* #1 of 1939, was filling in the missing half of the ancient equation with fire and water. Indeed, the Human Torch's battle against the Sub-Mariner in New York City was a retrieval of the ancient Chinese myth of the battle of Zhurong, the god of fire, with Gong Gong, the god of water. Just as they knock the cosmic mountain Buzhou off its axis, so the Human Torch and the Sub-Mariner knock the Empire State Building down. Together, then, all four characters are sigils which function to reconstruct the ancient theory of the four elements which Stan Lee and Jack Kirby will later consolidate into the Fantastic Four).

But opposing elements in bivalent ontologies often contain their opposites implicitly within them. Hence, the downward pointing triangle on Superman's chest is the ancient symbol for both water and earth (whereas air and fire are written orthographically as upward pointing triangles). The sigil on Batman's chest, on the other hand, features a winged animal. Each hero thus contains within himself the implicit possibility for appropriating the opposite power.

The signifiers of these superheroes, however, are not shifting and drifting like the floating signifiers of the post-metaphysical age. They are firmly anchored to their signifieds, creating a reassuringly firm cosmos of signifiers stitched to their quilting points in the signifieds which they refer to, unlike the cosmos of the mainstream culture which has come unglued and is full of signifiers that no longer refer to specific, stable signifieds. That is part of their appeal to the masses, this folklore of the urban proletariat, for it recalls the metaphysically certain world of the ancient religious traditions where the signifiers are nailed to their transcendental signifieds and do not threaten to slip underneath the worshipper's feet. The deconstructionist is not welcome in the world of comic book cosmologies, which has managed to be so popular precisely because it has preserved and miniaturized the ancient world of the metaphysical age as a sort of miniature terrarium in which heroes are precisely what they appear to be and bad guys like the Joker and Lex Luthor are *always* and irredeemably evil.

Notice that, whereas Lex Luthor is a scientist and therefore signifies Superman's disdain for the world of science and technology (Heidegger for the masses), the Joker is precisely a *riddler*, one who mocks and ridicules Batman's primarily logical mentality. Batman is a man of science, like Lex Luthor, whereas the Joker is the trickster figure who unsettles all metaphysical certainties with laughter, which upsets precisely because it unlocks the Pandora's Box wherein are contained ambiguities and polyvalent meanings that escape the overcoding of the rational consciousness structure. The Joker, in other words, is already threatening the rational and metaphysically certain cosmos of Batman with deconstruction; he is the French deconstructionist in disguise as a comic book super villain who is always threatening to come out of the box and take over Batman's metaphysical cosmos by overcoding it with skepticism and laughter, a laughter that overturns all values and renders them potentially meaningless. There is a direct line from Nietzsche to Derrida by way of the Joker.

And Batman knows this.

Superman, on the other hand, must save Lois Lane–that is to say, the human soul–from the machinations of technocrats and the men associated with Big Science who are always dreaming up schemes to trap and confine her with the tiny boxes of their evil design. Batman does not have an equivalent female figure to save, because he isn't trying to save humanity from anything except non-linearity. He is only defending the World City from dysfunctionality. As long as he can keep building his machines and ejecting entropy in the form of banishing his villains from the city of Gotham, he is contented. The smooth functioning of Gotham is all that matters. Superman is humanist; Batman is a technocrat.

So Superman and Batman are indeed as different from one another as day is from night. But whereas Batman is fighting to preserve civilization, Superman's point of view is more transcendental. He comes, after all, from another world entirely, a creature of Spirit opposed to matter, and he is a little more ambivalent about saving civilization. He comes with the memory of Other Worlds built innately into him, so he knows there are other possibilities for actualizing human life than just technocratic ones. It probably wouldn't matter much to him in the long run if Metropolis perished.

He would just take Lois Lane to live with him in his Fortress of Solitude at the North Pole. He would survive the end of civilization.

But Batman would go down with the ship.

Sixth Media Transformation: The Comic Book Phase II, The Marvel Renaissance

The Fantastic Four

According to the 19th century German poet Friedrich Holderlin, in his poem "Bread and Wine," the poet is one who "brings a trace of the fugitive gods / Down to the darkness of those who must live in their absence." For in that same poem, we contemporaries are imagined as having arrived "too late" for the gods, who have withdrawn from the stage of world history to the stars, from whence they gaze down at us with a certain cold indifference. They have, however, left behind for us a few signifiers, such as bread and wine, to remind us of their power and of the day of their inevitable return.

For Heidegger, the withdrawal of the gods was simultaneously tantamount to the ending of a world age–the metaphysical age in particular–and also the ending of a cycle of world history that began with the Greeks and came to its climax with Nietzsche. Heidegger saw us moderns as living in the time of the Between, that is to say, in the age of the world's darkening between two great cosmic cycles: the metaphysical age fading off into the temporal horizon behind us, and the second great age yet to come, in which the gods would return in a new *Ereignis* event that would result in the creation of new culture forms.[26]

But though the gods, ever since the nineteenth century, seem to have withdrawn from our cultural mainstream, they most definitely did not disappear altogether. In the writings of H.P. Lovecraft, for instance, we can already see them stirring and rumbling in the form of his great Leviathans awakening beneath the crags and rocky places of the world's abyssal regions–the ancient Titans, Asuras and Fomorians perhaps, on the turn of the spiral–while the heroes lived on, as we have seen in this book, in the pages of pulp fiction magazines and comic strips.

In 1961, with Stan Lee and Jack Kirby's creation of the comic book which they called *The Fantastic Four*, the gods can be found still surviving in the form of the various super villains who are imagined in issue after issue attacking the fabulous foursome, who are themselves a retrieval of the Aristotelian cosmology of the four elements. In the cosmology of matter that prevailed up until about the seventeenth century–with its revival of atomism–the physical world was thought to be comprised of the elements of earth, air, fire and water, and all things were interconvertible into each other if you knew the right proportions of the relation of hot and cold, wet and dry. It was the alchemist's job, for instance, to know these correct proportions and relations, so that he could transmute base metals into one or other of the nobler metals such as gold or silver. But with the rediscovery of the principle of all things being composed of atoms rather than elements, the elemental theory was transformed into chemistry as the Periodic Table, a theory based on number of electrons and atomic weight. The world picture of the four elements disintegrated.

The Fantastic Four, though, are human personifications of these elements: the Human Torch corresponding most obviously with fire; while the power of Invisibility of Sue Storm corresponds to air; and the brute force and strength of The Thing–

with his cracked earth physiognomy–corresponds to earth just as the ability of Reed Richards to assume any shape imitates the principle of liquidity, with its capacity to take on any form that it is poured into. The Four, then, represent a classic Jungian mandala, with their skyscraper headquarters in New York City, the Baxter Building, functioning as a kind of world axis in the dead center of the four that is analogous to the cosmic mountain in archaic mythologies, such as Mount Meru in Hindu myth. Thus, Marvel Comics survived, and was reborn, as the result of Lee and Kirby's miniaturization of archaic cosmology, which had long since disappeared from mainstream science and its enframing of the earth inside of a gigantic cage of machinery.

The first point to notice about the series is that the various attacks upon New York City, with the Four functioning as its obvious immune system, come from specific directions of the cosmic compass: the first attack, in the very first issue, comes from the World Below, in the form of the Mole Man, a subterranean dweller who lives with his armies of the sightless in the world beneath the earth. In later issues, he will attempt, time and again, to develop technologies which will enable him to attack the world's cities from below, even on occasion absconding with entire blocks of Manhattan, as in issue #31. He has a habit, too, of kidnapping Sue Storm, just like Pluto's theft of the maiden Persephone (or Ravana's of Sita in *The Ramayana*). And so indeed, we must regard him as the survival of the archaic Lord of the Underworld–Osiris, Hades, Satan–into comic book cosmology. He is also a villainous counterpart to the earth principle of Ben Grimm.

In issue #2, the attack comes from above, from the macrocosm of infinite space, with the Skrulls who descend from the stars with the capacity to shape-shift and assume the features of anyone. They are, of course, a holdover from the science fiction movies of the 1950s, such as *Invasion of the Body Snatchers*, but they also represent a displacement of the shape-shifting *rakshasa* or shamanic being from the hidden grottoes and arbors of the earth into the new cosmic canvas of outer space.

In issue #4, the attack comes, once again, from below, but this time from the sea in the form of the Sub-Mariner, or Prince Namor, a survivor from ancient Atlantis; but he is also a vestigial character left over from the Golden Age of Marvel Comics that flourished during the years of World War II, where he was the old nemesis of the Human Torch, a character who has carried over into the Marvel Renaissance from that same era. Namor (which is simply "roman" spelled backwards) is very obviously the god Neptune, or the Lord of the Watery Abyss (Varuna in ancient Vedic India, or Manannan MacLir in Celtic myth). In Chinese mythology, he would correspond to one of the various Dragon Kings who live beneath the world's oceans and govern its water circuits and manage its rain and river cycles.

In issue #5, the attack comes, not from below or above but as it were, horizontally from the world of Old Europe in the form of Doctor Doom, one of the four's most persistent villains, for he represents the Faustian principle of Old European science that was never fully disentangled from the world of occult practices and whose final, decayed vision was exemplified by the Nazis. (Doctor Doom, in essence, is Faust himself, scaled down and miniaturized for mass consumption. His Man in the Iron Mask costume marks him, furthermore, as a survivor from the Old World of feudalistic Europe). He too, though, is elemental, for in Chinese mythology, his armored exoskeleton would correspond to the principle of metal, one of the five basic Chinese elements. As a scientist, he is the nemesis in particular of Reed Richards who, on the other hand, represents the J. Robert Oppenheimer type of American approach to science as a committee working on behalf of impersonal corporate-military institutions (whereas Doom is the type of mad-scientist as loner).

And so, with Doctor Doom and the Skrulls (who, as in *Invasion of the Body Snatchers* are also a cipher for the Reds, who might dwell amongst us in disguise as friendly neighbors), and with the Mole Man and the Sub-Mariner, the Four find their most persistent adversaries as resurrected gods and heroes of the metaphysical and mythical ages. These villains, furthermore, signify the old archaic world of locally-bound and cosmologically enclosed spheres. Indeed, they represent the principle of sphere-building itself, for they are always trying to capture, cover, enclose or separate Manhattan from the rest of the world, which is precisely the function of archaic mythologies: such mythologies "presence" very specific world horizons (usually localized as one or another cosmic world city, such as Chang'an in China or Ayodhya in ancient India) as *Ereignis* events that make worlds "world" (or resonate) in the Heideggerian sense, which is to say that they make the near near and the far far precisely by "thinging," like Heidegger's proverbial bridge across the river that "gathers" together his fourfold of earth and sky, mortals and divinities.[27] Ancient mythologies, that is, create enclosures, boundaries and spheres that wrap and seal local horizons off from the rest of the world "out there," and in the process, they sanctify the local and cast the provincial into the realm of the profane.

In this sense, the gods of the Old World differ significantly from the gods of contemporary hypermodernity, for the Fantastic Four–as one such example of these new gods–are the immune system of an *open* universe that has emerged from out of the smoking ruins of World War II: a horizonless world *without* spherical enclosures or domes of any kind, a world that is open to all other worlds, including the infinite space of the macrocosm. It is a "cosmos" that has the very interesting and very new characteristic of being permanently "open" to all other worlds: since it has no enclosures of any kind, the job of the Fantastic Four isn't simply to defend Manhattan as its immune system, but to *prevent* enclosures of any kind from coming down around this new open universe, just as the function of myth and religion in the metaphysical and mythical world ages was to invent such enclosures.

For world-enclosure is tantamount to the erection of metaphysical systems that close down all horizons by capturing them and binding them within a single metaphysically-certain worldview that isolates them from all others, and opposes all others in the process. That was the essence of the metaphysical age: "our metaphysics is mightier than yours," ran its mantra, and this became the basis for wars and genocides of all kinds.

So, the job of the Fantastic Four, in other words, is *to keep the universe open at all costs,* for the world order of capital is an open horizon within which the circulation of goods and services in the planetary ecumene must be allowed to proceed. Its cosmology (in the sense of physics) too, is open, for there are no longer any world enclosing domes surrounding the earth, and as a result it is ontologically open and listening to the stars for the possibility of encounters with new entities. Who knows who, or what else out there might be converted to the religion of trade and commerce?

Thus, as the series evolves, this resistance to the principle of bondage and enclosure becomes more and more pronounced as a theme. Beginning in issue #36, for instance, the Fantastic Four encounter a shadow version of themselves called the "Frightful Four," a group of three (male) criminals known as the Wizard, their mastermind, who is the shadow version of Reed Richards; The Sandman, one of Spider-Man's villains, who is the shadowy counterpart of Ben Grimm, the earth principle; and The Trapster, who has no exact counterpart, for his power is the ability to use tiny gadgets and guns to build traps that capture people and freeze and arrest their ability to move about. The female member of the group, and hence, a loose counterpart to Sue Storm, is Medusa, a woman with fiery red hair that seems to have its own life and can reach out in tentacular fashion to grab and seize anyone. They all wear purple suits, significantly, for whereas the Fantastic Four wear blue suits, the color of the daytime sky and hence of expansiveness, purple is the color of twilight and hence, signifies the descent of the dome of the nighttime sky.

The Fantastic Four battle the Frightful Four in issue after issue, finally meeting a nemesis which they are simply unable to defeat. For whereas the elemental powers of the Fantastic Four are expansive and cosmic, the powers of the Frightful Four are contractive and based upon binding, seizing, capturing and arresting physical motion. (The Wizard, who corresponds to Reed Richards, has the power of using anti-gravity discs to suspend an individual's ability to move about the surface of the earth). The God Who Binds, however, was a notable characteristic-identified in particular by the comparative mythologist Mircea Eliade–of a certain type of god in the mythical age. In India, this was the very ancient god known as Varuna, a sea god associated with snakes and nagas, and one of whose attributes was to carry a rope that was normally used to capture, punish and bind people[28] (The Trapster, whose paste gun is attached to his hip via a sort of cord, corresponds to him perfectly). Varuna was a god of the macrocosm, associated with destiny forces such as *rta*, as Eliade remarks, and therefore represents the principle of Fate and Karma: those forces which capture the soul, bind it, and lock it into place in the world of matter. The Archons of Gnostic cosmology had a similar function, for they captured the human soul with cosmic fatalism, trapping it into matter as it descended through each planetary sphere toward its incarnation on the earth below, where the hapless soul was doomed to whatever fate the Archons had inscribed onto it.

And so the battle of the Fantastic Four against the Frightful Four is, on the one hand, the battle of the rational, scientific worldview against the cosmic fatalism of astrology and the ancients. But it is also the battle to keep open and maintain the Clearing of the Open Universe of hypermodernity, in which all viewpoints are tolerated and welcomed and no metaphysically certain thought systems are allowed to capture and limit its possibilities.

Medusa herself, however–the most interesting of the Frightful Four–is a member, as it turns out, of an ancient race known as the Inhumans, a race not of mutants but of beings with superpowers who are older than humanity and have largely remained hidden from it. Their attitude toward humans is one of paranoia, for they have withdrawn into a secret island hideaway known as the Great Refuge which is pictured, unsurprisingly, as an enclosed dome. The world of ancient myth and tradition is precisely the world of domical enclosures demarcating boundary membranes between one civilization as over against another. The various wars and violent acts of history–the Maccabean Revolt, for instance, or the Battle of Tours or Marathon–are boundary acts in which the metaphysical immune system of one society rubs up against that of another. The resulting friction is violence.

And then, in issue #48, we encounter Lee and Kirby's crown jewel of Fantastic Four writing: "The Coming of Galactus." For the first time, the Four encounter a villain against which they are simply powerless, for Galactus is a giant being who has come from some murky corner of the universe, arriving in his spaceship to the roof of the Baxter Building where he begins to assemble a mechanical device for sucking up all the earth's etheric energy. Galactus is a devourer of worlds (like Shiva) and he has found the earth as the result of sending forth his herald the Silver Surfer, a man who surfs the cosmos at light speed looking for fresh planetary victims to nourish his master, the great god-like Galactus. But the Fantastic Four have been warned by another giant being known as the Watcher–a being who has been stationed on the moon and is not allowed to intervene in history, but merely to observe it–who explains to them that they are powerless against Galactus, although the Watcher knows of an all-powerful device that can be fetched from another dimension and used to stop him with the threat of total cosmic annihilation. Thus, the Watcher sends the Human Torch through a kind of cosmic wormhole to retrieve the device (and note that, in this role, the Torch is in relation to the Watcher exactly as the Silver Surfer is in relation to Galactus, for the Surfer corresponds as a spiritual being of the air to the Human Torch, whose fiery principle links him to the Spirit). Meanwhile, the Silver Surfer has fallen in love with Ben Grimm's blind girlfriend, Alicia, and has decided that humans might be worth preserving after all. He attempts to stop Galactus in an apocalyptic battle that takes place in the skies above Manhattan, until the Torch returns with the all-powerful device–a device small enough to be held in the hand and so, like the atom bomb, is out of all proportion to its destructive power–that is then used to threaten the very existence of Galactus, who finally relents. But take note that the Four were only able to defeat Galactus at the behest of the Watcher. They could have done nothing against him on their own.

The entire episode, though, has the feel of a retrieval and miniaturization of the ancient Sumerian descent of the gods to the tops of their ziggurats. The Watcher, with his bald head, even resembles the bald-headed and clean-shaven Sumerian priests who ascended the great stairways to the top of their ziggurats where they prepared, in ritual and liturgical recitation, for the descent to earth of one or another of their great gods. And even the headgear which Galactus wears, with two horns sticking out of the sides of his helmet, is similar to the horned headgear that the Sumerians imagined to be worn by their gods.

Thus, the ultimate, and primordial, ritual, that is, which brought civilization into being in the first place–the descent of the gods to the cities that were founded specifically to worship them–is here captured, miniaturized and rejected by Lee and Kirby as incompatible with the world order of the global capitalist ecumene. The Great Ritual, too, is a ritual that brings down a god, and hence an enclosure of metaphysical certainty, around one's local city. Each of the Sumerian cities was a world unto itself whose ziggurats were landing pads for the god specific to that city. Each city was metaphysically self-certain through being held in bondage to a specific god: Uruk, for instance, was sacred to Inanna and her father An, while Ur was sacred to the moon god Nanna-Sin, and Nippur to Enlil, and so on. These cities, consequently, frequently went to war with each other, like the Greek city-states, as ways of testing which one the gods favored most.

Thus, the mythical and metaphysical ages of Enclosure, after World War II, are over. The Fantastic Four was invented by Lee and Kirby in 1961 not just to provide New York with an immune system, but specifically to defend the world order of capital and to prevent enclosure and metaphysical certainty from capturing it and surrounding it. *All* enclosures are rejected by the Fantastic Four. All metaphysical certainties–save those of science, which is the only allowable way in which entities are permitted to unconceal themselves in this new world order–together with the gods who sanctify them, are anathematized and cleared away so that capital may function inside of a world space that is cleared of gods and astral spirits with their limiting and confining functions. No signifiers are allowed, any longer, to be anchored to specific locales. All signifiers in the capitalist world space must be allowed to freely circulate in orbit across the globe, just like the astronauts must be given free roam in orbit about the earth, for this is the age of orbiting signifiers: Buddhist chapels in California and Boulder; Russian Orthodox churches in Pittsburgh; mosques in New York and London; *all* signifiers have become free-floating and must be allowed to circulate freely through global space.[29]

It is the job of the Fantastic Four to keep that global space clear and free of obstructions, so that the signifiers of the past, signifiers which once bound themselves to resonate at specific localities–Things thinging so that worlds could "world" in the sense of Heidegger–can now be free to roam, drift and circulate like debris in orbit about the earth.

Thus, each of the cosmologically bounding world functions of super villains like the Mole Man (who wishes to pull cities down into his subterranean kingdom), or the Sub-Mariner (who wishes to flood them), or Doctor Doom (who is ever inventing new traps with which to capture them and put them like models of ships inside of bottles), must be defeated, resisted and overthrown. No longer is it an age of localized gods of this or that under- or upper- world sanctifying particular places and cities of the earth by drawing membranes around them and cosmic domes over them. All cities, and all worlds, must remain open, free and clear to the circulation of capital and the global free flow of proliferating signifiers.

That is the task of the Fantastic Four.

Spider-Man

Spider-Man is, of course, thoroughly immunological, like the Fantastic Four or Batman, but unlike them his totem icon is the spider, and this means that he is creating webs to trap astral spirits and beings and keep them out of the city. If the Fantastic Four make up the city's cosmological infrastructure–dealing with beings from vast reaches of outer space–Spider-Man's focus is a little more narrow: he is Manhattan's liver, secreting enzymes to capture and filter out toxic elements. The villains that he battles, moreover, are for the most part symbols left over from the mythological age of the soul's microcosmology.

As Jean Gebser pointed out in his *Ever-Present Origin*, the history of the soul has been one of a gradual narrowing and simplification of its functions, paralleling the gradual scaling down and shearing away of the gods in the process of monotheism.[30] Aboriginals speak of thousands of souls, and in Old Kingdom Egypt, the pharaoh was thought to have fourteen *ka*'s. Later on, in the Middle Kingdom, he has one *ka*, one *ba*, a *khaibit*, a *renn* soul, and himself comprises a *sahu*, that is to say, a shining one among the stars. By the time of Plato, furthermore, the number of souls has been sheared down to just three: an animal soul, a vegetative soul and a rational soul, while in India, there still reigned the micro-polytheism of the various sheaths: the *anna-maya-kosha*, the *prana-maya-kosha*, and so on, boxes within boxes like Russian dolls.

In Biblical times, there are also only three components: the body, and the indwelling psyche that animates it, and then the *pneuma* or spirit soul that descends down from the heavens into a man like Samson and renders him capable of great deeds. Thus, the gradual creation of a simplified monotheistic soul has taken place in parallel with the actual creation of monotheism by Akhenaten, Moses and their Hebrew descendants. Nowadays we speak merely of *the* soul.

By the time of the comic book cosmologies of New York in the 1960s, however, all this is coming undone: the entire history of the soul's monotheism is splintering apart into a thousand tiny filaments and squirming, wriggling microsouls that have escaped from their envelopes of semiotic capture and gone running amok throughout the city. With the collapse of the Transcendental Signifieds (God, the Soul, Freedom, etc.) holding them in place anymore, the soul's polytheism has reverted back to its original and primordial anarchy. It is Spider-Man's task, specifically as a spinner of webs, to create a new apparatus of capture with new filaments that will hold them in place again, just like the lines of the great web of stars that hold the constellations in place in the heavens. He doesn't *consciously* realize what he is doing, of course (superheroes seldom ever do) but he *is* a monotheist in disguise, gathering up the anarchistic elements of escaped soul components and weaving them back together into their ancient unity. He is therefore a direct descendant of figures like King Josiah or Theodosius the Great, capturing, hammering and destroying the icons of polytheism with ardent Western zealotry.

Consider, for instance, Spider-Man's battle with the Vulture in *The Amazing Spider-Man* #2 (and then again in #7). The

Vulture is a bald man with a beak-like nose who wears a green vulture outfit that enables him to fly through the air using some sort of magnetic field. He is, in other words, simply the archaic image (a *very* ancient image) of the human-headed birdman. In ancient Egypt, this was the component of the soul known as the Ba, often depicted in funerary art as a human-headed bird hovering above the mummified *sahu*. The Ba can leave the mummified body and travel out at night into the astral plane, but it always returns in the daytime. The Ba is also found in ancient Sumerian art, painted onto the side of chariots that have been buried with the dead, for the Sumerians liked to imagine their dead as birdmen in the underworld. And Greek mythology is full of human-headed bird creatures like Harpies and Sirens.

But note their funerary context: they represent what Jean Gebser terms the "soul's death pole,"[31] which is associated with air and with winged beings such as angels. Spider-Man's foe, that is, has escaped from the rubbish heap of the mythological age, and it is the task of Spider-Man to capture him with his web and put him back in his place.

In *The Amazing Spider-Man* #3, we are first introduced to one of Spider-Man's most famous villains: Dr. Octopus, the man who has a set of four mechanical arms sutured to his body as the result of an atomic accident. The association with the octopus marks him as a type of modified water creature and therefore is to be identified with the opposite component of the soul, the "soul's life pole," as Gebser puts it,[32] which is always identified with watery elements and creatures. The Muses, for instance, or any kind of fish creatures, such as the Babylonian fish god Enki, who had a sacred cult of well-springs associated with him that was particularly popular on the island of Bahrein (where he was there known as Inzag). (Indeed, this cult may have stretched all the way down the Persian Gulf and around the corner to Mohenjo-daro, which had the famous baptismal bath associated with it). The soul's life pole is often depicted as the ferryman who pilots the craft that takes one down the River Styx and off into the underworld.

But the octopus was a common animal depicted on Minoan and Mycenaean vases from the second millennium BC. They are common on double-handled vases from around 1200 BC, and in the mythologies associated with them, they are thought to represent the principle of darkness that strangles the light and the sun as it attempts to emerge from the watery abyss. The snaky hair of the Medusa may have been inspired by this idea of the octopus that can freeze and arrest motion simply by tackling it with all its arms.

So, in either case, we have the Vulture as an archaic survival of an instance of the soul's death pole, and the octopus as a survival of the soul's life pole (though it is a version that portends death, so it is an ambivalent image). These are signifiers once associated with the architecture of the subtle body, but now they have escaped capture and come loose, running about the city as floating signifiers with no apparatus of capture to hold them in place.

The Lizard Man, too, which Spider-Man encounters in *The Amazing Spider-Man* #8, is the ancient dragon-serpent in disguise. He is the lower evolutionary brain, the reptilian brain stem that forms the basis for all higher transformations of consciousness. He would correspond to Rudolf Steiner's astral body, that component of the subtle body which simply represents pure animalistic consciousness with a nervous system. (In the ancient sagas of the Narts, the Lizard Man–Arkhon Arkhoz–captures the maiden Psatina and takes her to the underworld).[33]

But in any event, it is evident that all these components of the subtle microtecture of the soul have come unglued; the elements are undergoing a reverse monotheism and they are proliferating much faster, issue by issue, than Spider-Man can even get a grip on them. His task, then, as a spinner of webs is to create a new architecture, a new apparatus of semiotic capture within which to house these escaped components of the contemporary disintegrating soul. In Islamic tradition, the Spider's House is a delicate thing, indeed, but it is, after all, sticky enough to hold the constellations in place in the night sky, and so that is exactly Spider-Man's task: to use the web of fate, karma and destiny to put all these escaped zoo animals back into their respective places in the heavens, where they will snap back into place on the inside of the soul's microtecture, as well.

The spider as a mythological creature is typically, though not always, female, because she represents the Web of Fate: the Norns–in Germanic myth–or the Moirae in Greek myth, whose names are Atropos, Clotho and Lachesis, the ones who measure out, spin and cut the thread of a human life. They are essentially a three-fold spider goddess weaving the subtle body of a man's incarnational vessel. But note that they also form the "texture" or "textile" of the woven threads that hold all its components in place: the death pole, the life pole, the brain stem, etc.

Thus, Spider-Man is a creature of Fate whose job is to weave the soul's tapestry as a textile upon which all its signifiers will be embroidered and encoded. But in the age of disintegrating semiotic systems, he has a huge task in front of him, since all the soul's ancient components have escaped capture and broken free, where they are racing out across the walls and spires of the skyscrapers of Gotham.

His web, therefore, must remain forever incomplete. It is the equivalent of an unfinished work of postmodernity, like one of Kafka's novels, that simply *cannot* be completed due to the enormity of the task of gathering up all the escaped signifiers.

Rebuilding the West's devolved soul-apparatus is, then, the task of Spider-Man, as a pop culture icon. In this sense, he is the opposite of a French deconstructionist, whose task is to pull such systems apart, like pulling the legs off of an insect and letting it lie there, squirming.

Spider-Man is racing feverishly, working around the clock, to put back together the very apparatuses of semiotic capture which the French deconstructionists have dismantled.

Seventh Media Transformation:
The Postwar Paperback Novel

James Bond

Planetary Hero

The first James Bond novel, Ian Fleming's *Casino Royale*, appeared in 1953, just as the Korean War was coming to an end and the C.I.A. was planning the removal of Mossadegh from office in Iran. Within a few years, the U.S. government would begin sending U-2 spy planes on reconnaissance missions over Moscow, to which the Russians would respond by imprisoning the entire planet within the orbit of the world's first satellite, *Sputnik*. Thus, in the world into which Fleming's famous character was born, everyone was busy looking over everyone else's shoulders. Indeed, Bond himself is essentially an extension of the human eyeball, cut loose from the body and sent roving across the planet to peer through walls and behind closed doors. If the Berlin Wall was Russia's response to the Marshall Plan, then the West's response to the Berlin Wall was James Bond, a man who specializes in boring through walls.

The job of the artist, as Marshall McLuhan was fond of saying, is to make invisible environments visible–that is, to retrieve environments that have sunken below the threshold of perception because of their very omnipresence–and this is certainly true of the James Bond mythos, which casts an X-ray upon the paranoid environment created by the global surveillance technologies of the Cold War. In the early Sean Connery films, we often see Bond checking into a hotel room, and the first thing he does is to scan the room for signs of electronic surveillance, peering behind lampshades or looking underneath telephones or inside of closets. Prior to the Cold War, such behavior would have been proof of a man's insanity, but *within* the environment structured by the new surveillance technologies, what would previously have been regarded as mental illness is now indicative of the highest mental alertness. Thus Bond, like Nixon after him, is a paranoid, and his behavior anticipates in fiction what will become a reality under the Nixon administration, in which wiretapping, burglaries, and the Xeroxing of classified documents become *de rigeur* components of government.

Of course, there have always been spies, and so governments have always been paranoid to a degree, but in a world in which the *entire planet* has come under surveillance with light speed technologies, this nervous anxiety is stepped up to a level of intensity bordering on the hysterical. So it is no wonder that gunshots, car chases and explosions compose the fabric of Bond's everyday life, for his consciousness is perpetually flooded with adrenalin and therefore lodged into a permanent fight or flight mode. Hence, his need for constant sexual gratification is almost his only means of discharging such excess nervous energy.

But of course, no one could ever actually *live* the way James Bond does, for he would soon enough collapse into insanity and nervous exhaustion, like the protagonist of Steven Spielberg's *Munich,* based upon a real life spy story. The Bond mythos, however, is not a portrait study, but rather a caricature drawn large enough to make a point. And the point, it seems to me, is that it is *human beings* who shape history, not impersonal institutions and bureaucracies. According to the ancient canon of aesthetics which prevailed up until the discovery of perspectival space in the Renaissance, the largest figures upon a canvas–like the Virgin Mary or Christ–were indicative of those with the most importance attached to them. What is less important–in Medieval art, such things as landscapes and buildings, items which will become the very center of revelation during the later perspectival epoch–is sloughed off as so much background noise. Thus, with James Bond, the development that began in Renaissance art with Brueghel the Elder's *Procession to Calvary* (1564)–in which three dimensional visual space has so enveloped the field of awareness that it has swallowed up Christ to the point where he has vanished amongst the crowd and can barely be discerned–has been entirely reversed, for if the Bond character looms so impossibly large, it is because he has stepped outside the containing walls of real, three dimensional space, and into the strangely distorted and weirdly elongated world of the light speed hero.

Oral Heroes / Literate Heroes

That Bond is a two-dimensional figure, there can be no doubt. He is one of those iconic heroes of our electronic society who are moving so quickly through the system that they have collapsed, like an object approaching light speed, into two-dimensionality. Bond is as flat as a credit card.

But then the world in which Bond lives and breathes is not the one which you and I inhabit. His world is a resonant, echoing cavern populated by mythological beings disguised as spies, counterspies and assassins. For at the speed of light, the world collapses into the two-dimensionality of mythic archetypes and masked, tribal heroes. These beings are two-dimensional because their masks have the effect of absorbing the 3D personality of the real human individual. When our children dress up for Halloween, they are instantly vanishing into the ghostly world of tribal man, for their costumes depersonalize them as they disappear into another, flatter dimension. A dimension in which Time as we know it does not exist, but always *is*, and never *was*.

Consider, for instance, the fact that in James Bond movies, there are never any children or, with few exceptions, any elderly people (the exceptions are M, his boss, and Q, his weapons specialist, but these are the tribal elders whose presence, in order to direct Bond's violence into rational channels, is required). Try as he will, the viewer will be lucky indeed to spot the presence of a child in a James Bond film. Oh, they're there, of course, in some of the background shots. But the fact that one must squint to see them proves my point. And the point is that in the Bond universe, Time is the enemy, just as it was for Plato. There are no children and there are no old people because the Bond world is not one that admits of the presence of Becoming.

Take the typical Bond villain. This is the one consistent exception to the rule that there are no old people, because almost without exception, the Bond villain is an old– or at least, late middle-aged–man. Old Age, in other words, *is* the villain in the Bond films, and in defeating crippled old men time and again, Bond is eliminating Father Time from his world. This is also why there are no unattractive women in the Bond universe, because to admit the presence of an ugly woman would be an affront to the realm of Eternal Forms in which Bond lives and breathes. Only beauties are allowed because beautiful women are *young* women. Old Age is thus denied once again, along with the imperfections of ugliness. Plato was quite intolerant of imperfections in his ideal realm of the Forms, which he identified with the heavens, while the earth, as in the Christian cosmos, was fallen and corrupt. The Bond films, then, occupy the same universe as that of Plato's Forms and so in the film version of *Moonraker* we are not surprised to see Bond finally ascend into outer space, for the heavens constitute the Platonist's ultimate goal.

The world of James Bond is also, to a certain extent, a retrieval of the orally transmitted world of tribal man, in which the hero never dies or, if he does, like Lemminkainen in the *Kalevala* or the title character of the *Mwindo Epic*, always returns, like a television show, for next week's installment. For the world of tribal man occupies an acoustically resonant space in which the principle of mnemonic repetition takes the place of the written storage of knowledge. Knowledge that does not have a basis for its existence in writing must be stored in the memory through the accentuation of repetitive factors. Hence, the narratives of tribal epics like *Sundiata: an Epic of Old Mali* or the *Mwindo Epic* do not have much in the way of a story line, but are composed of episodic repetitions of events with slight variations. Mwindo's fight with his father Shemwindo, for instance, is reduplicated in the episode of his fight with Mukiti, the serpent man, and then again later on in the underworld, with Muisa, the god of the dead, and once again at the end with Dragon. Each episode is but a variation on itself, with Mwindo always emerging triumphant.[34] And in *Sundiata*, the characters are strongly polarized, as they tend to be in the Bond sagas, for one is either on the side of Sundiata–who is attempting to win back his kingdom of Mali–or on the side of his evil magician nemesis Soumarou, who has the disquieting ability to appear and disappear upon the field of battle. There is no in between.[35]

These are some of the many characteristics which the postliterate world of the light speed–and hence, electric–hero shares in common with the pre-literate world of tribal man. Narrative forms under electric conditions have the paradoxical effect of reversing their protagonists back into mythic, tribal beings with mask-like characteristics. This explains why the actors who have played Bond most successfully are the ones with faces that closely resemble masks: Sean Connery's face is capable of only one or two expressions at most; Roger Moore's twinkling eyes shine out from behind an otherwise rigid, featureless visage; Pierce Brosnan's face resembles that of a department store mannikin's; and Daniel Craig's chiseled granite features are perhaps the most mask-like of them all. (An actor like Harrison Ford, by contrast, could never have played Bond convincingly, for his face is far too animated with wry grimaces, sarcastic expressions and bemusement). The epithets, furthermore, that are typically assigned to the characters of tribal epics ("clever Odysseus"; "wise Nestor"; or Mwindo's "Little One Just Born He Walked") as stock formulae of oral mnemonics find their echo in Bond's characteristic "shaken, not stirred," or his self identification as "Bond. James Bond." (The Shadow's laugh was a similar acoustic signifier on radio).

However, that the Bond stories share these characteristics with the narratives of pre-literate thought does not mean that they are simply a reversion to oral tradition, for there is a difference between the post-literate mentality of our electronic "orality" and the pre-literate mentality of oral cultures in that post-literate narratives depend for their existence upon writing and bear the traces of its existence within them. They are, for one thing, generally tightly plotted, which is a characteristic not normally found in oral narratives with their rambling, meandering episodes that may or may not add up to what literates would regard as a good story. The first tightly plotted narratives, as Walter Ong has shown, were the product of the Greek theater, and these were narratives controlled by writing, the first such verbal narratives to have their origin in a society that was becoming literate[36]. A Westerner who attempts to wade through the many volumes of an orally based Hindu epic like the *Mahab-*

harata or the *Ramayana* is in for a surprise, since the Hindus, as a traditionally oral culture, take so many narrative detours from the plots of these epics that it requires them multiple volumes to ever get around to actually telling the main story. Westerners become frustrated with this sort of oral A.D.D. very quickly and so tend to put the volumes aside after reading only the first one or two of them.

The Bond universe, with all its weird properties of temporal negation and spatial distortion, is the product of a complex culture in which writing, orality and electronics have all been superimposed upon one another to create narrative forms that are too distinctly oral to be labeled "literate," but yet too "literate" to be truly a product of an oral mentality. Instead, these narratives lie somewhere in between.

The Bond Formula

That the Bond universe is an essentially acoustic world governed by the principles of reverberation and resonance is also confirmed by a study of the morphology of the typical Bond narrative. After reading a number of the Ian Fleming paperback novels, or watching a handful of the movies, it becomes rather easy to see that they are almost invariably rehearsals of the same pattern reiterated tirelessly with formulaic repetition from film to film (or novel to novel, as the case may be). And what is this basic morphology?

With few variations, the pattern typically manifests itself in the following way:

After an action-filled prologue, Bond is summoned to a meeting with an irritable M, who is always on the verge of firing him, but decides to send him on a mission anyway (in the later Bond movies with Timothy Dalton and Pierce Brosnan, this scene begins to drift further on into the film, usually after the first half hour or so);

Bond sets out on the mission, and almost immediately ends up in a mano a mano fight with an eccentric henchman;

At some point within the film's first third, he meets his female sidekick (sometimes his nemesis), who usually has a silly name ("Pussy Galore," "Solitaire," "Good Night," "Onnatop;" etc.) and with whom he is destined to sleep, but not to commit emotionally, for to commit emotionally to a woman would be a concession to the real 3D world in which the soul falls and becomes caught in the antagonistic pleasure of erotic entanglements;

Bond soon encounters the villain, who is almost always *an old man* who has designed some kind of a mechanical or electronic *system* with which he intends to subvert world order;

This evil old man usually has a colorful sidekick / henchman: a dwarf (*The Man With the Golden Gun*); a giant with steel jaws (*The Spy Who Loved Me*); a hat-throwing assassin (*Goldfinger*); a tall, black Amazonian woman (*A View to a Kill*) etc. This henchman is Bond's primary nemesis throughout the course of each particular film;

The narrative concludes with a showdown at the evil old man's Fortress of Solitude, which is invariably located in some remote, bizarre, or out of the way place, such as in an extinct volcano (*You Only Live Twice*); on a remote island (*Dr. No* and *The Man With the Golden Gun*); in the middle of the ocean (*The Spy Who Loved Me*); at the top of a mountain (*On Her Majesty's Secret Service* and *For Your Eyes Only*); in the jungles of Cuba (*Goldeneye*); etc. (*The Living Daylights* is notable for containing only a vestigial echo of this sequence in the rather brief scene which occurs *after* the film's climax, in which Bond fights with the arms dealer named Whitaker inside of his private mansion).

During this final showdown, Bond's female sidekick is taken captive, or else has already been taken captive earlier in the narrative, and now Bond must rescue her;

The Fortress of Solitude is destroyed, usually by explosions, and the evil old man killed;

In the film's coda, Bond ends up making love with his female sidekick, which is the last we ever see of her because she never returns in any of the sequels.

Now, the mystery here is why, after over forty-five years of watching the same film with the same basic storyline, audiences are *still* willing to pay to see the latest James Bond film (as of this writing, the most recent entry was *Spectre*). This is surely unique in the annals of film history, for there is no other example of a single character who becomes the protagonist of a movie every other year for over five decades. This means that there is a psychological significance to the Bond Formula, since everyone who goes to see a James Bond film knows *exactly* what they're going to get, and yet they still go anyway.

Now, myth is an inherently conserving force. It acts within the psyche as a kind of crystal which keeps its form while weathering change. Within the field of culture as a whole, the function of myth is to stabilize a society against the disintegrative effects that are wreaked upon it by technological transformations (at least, that is its function *nowadays*). And to watch all twenty Bond films in chronological order (or to read the books) is to review a catalogue of the unfolding of technological inventions over the latter half of the twentieth century. But as the new machines keep coming, Bond just takes them up into his metabolism and assimilates them through the pure act of mythic repetition. That is to say, the very repetition of his *actions* while the technological environment around him is constantly changing is the whole appeal of the Bond films (albeit unconsciously) to the audiences that keep going back for more. The Bond films provide the public with an example of the constancy and stability of a mythic structure that is capable of withstanding the disruptive effects of the impact of new technologies. While the outer world around Bond changes, Bond himself does not.

The message, then, to the viewer is: you must not let yourself be intimidated by these gadgets, for they cannot affect the essential stability of your humanity. So the public keeps going to see these films because they are curious about how good old Bond–his age kept perpetually the same by casting him anew every decade or so–will respond to *this* year's gadgets.

The Bond stories, as I have said, are all about how the human individual–greatly magnified to emphasize his importance (witness the opening fight sequence of the 2006 film *Casino Royale*, in which a backdrop of huge construction machinery is somehow dwarfed by the intensity of the man to man combat) retains his humanity in a world in which that very humanity is constantly threatened by the Machine. Bond will *not* capitulate to the Machine: this is the point of his confrontation with the old man villain who has mastered some technological system with which he threatens the world.

Instead, he has metabolized the Machine, for in the films, he literally absorbs machinery into his body. Time after time, we witness his escape from one tight squeeze after the next due to some tiny gadget or device which seems to emerge spontaneously from his very anatomy: in the heel of a boot, he finds some electronic component, or his watch contains a laser, or an innocuous pen is used as a bomb, etc. Bond, then, is a mythic being who has made the Machine serve *him* and not the other way around. He uses machines as extensions of his own anatomy and does not allow them to interfere with the functioning of his personality–such as it is.

Bond is *larger* than the Megamachine.

Global Hero

In my book *Celluloid Heroes & Mechanical Dragons*, I pointed out that the comic book superhero functions like an immune cell designed to protect the modern atheistic metropolis from incursions out of the world of myth and symbol.[37] The noir hero, likewise, from Sherlock Holmes to Sam Spade, protects a particular metropolis from attacks by mythical beings. With James Bond, however, we are not dealing with any sort of immune system at all, for Bond, unlike those other heroes, is not tied to any specific city, not even London, despite his working for the British Secret Service. For Bond is, in fact, *the first global superhero of popular literature*. Any given Bond narrative, that is to say, can be set now in Japan, now in Germany or India, Hong Kong or Las Vegas. He is thus the first pop hero to presuppose the *entire world* as his stage, and so he is intimately linked with the global order brought into being during the Cold War.

The character of James Bond, then, is no immune cell defending one country against another, or a single city from the attacks of mythic beings, for on the contrary, *Bond is himself an antigen* working like a virus to attach himself to the cell wall of this or that systemic apparatus in order to disrupt its functioning *from within*, exactly like a virus does to the cell that it destroys. Bond is forever puncturing the cell walls of enemy systems and causing them to become sick or ill. In the climax of one narrative after the next, we see him penetrating the interior of the villain's stronghold: in *Dr. No*, for instance–the first of the movies (1962)–he passes, together with his female sidekick, over a threshold into No's fortress where he soon brings the place down with the usual fire and destruction. In Fleming's novel *Casino Royale*, Bond is given the assignment of humiliating the KGB operative Le Chiffre at a game of cards inside a Monte Carlo-like resort. He enters into this resort and, after beating the asthmatic Le Chiffre at cards, causes him to sweat, as though he had actually entered *inside* Le Chiffre's body and given him a fever. But Le Chiffre, in an allergic reaction, as it were, expels Bond from his body and has him taken captive, bound and gagged, to his mansion where he tortures him almost to death. At the climax of the movie *For Your Eyes Only*, we witness Bond scaling the precipitous cliff wall of a monastery within which the villain has taken up residence, and into which Bond enters and destroys the fortress with explosives.

Bond, then, is a capitalist virus blown about the globe, sent searching for warm enemy bodies to infect. And the villains within whose bodies he finds himself lodged, moreover, are often beings and characters out of ancient myth. In *Dr. No*, for instance, we are presented with a villain who has a pair of mechanical hands and whose goal is the creation of a special type of radioactive device which will disrupt electronic operations, specifically, the West's attempts to launch rockets into space. In Hindu mythology, likewise, the *asuras* and *rakshasas* are forever attempting to sabotage the priestly performance of the fire sacrifice that enables the *brahmins* to ascend into the heavens and commune with the gods. Indeed, the description of the demon king Ravana that we find in the *Ramayana* could apply just as well to Dr. No: "A breaker of laws he would violate the wives of other men, and use any unearthly weapon to obstruct the sacrifice."[38] In the *Shatapatha Brahmana*, we find the *asuras* attempting to build their own ladder to heaven by creating a duplicate copy of a fire altar, piling brick upon brick up toward the sky, but the god Indra disrupts this activity by pulling out the central brick and causing the whole thing to collapse. Indra's role here is essentially the same as Bond's vis a vis the villains that he fights, for he, too, is a monster slayer like Rama or Thor or Zeus, who has traded in his thunderbolt for a Walther PPK (Q, the man who supplies him with all his weapons, corresponds to the blacksmith divinity who normally creates the dragon slayer's thunderbolts and tridents: thus Koshar wa Hasis, who makes the thunderbolts for Baal in Canaanite myth; or the Cyclopes who manufacture Zeus's thunderbolts during his war against the Titans; or the smith god Tvastr who makes Indra's *vajra* for him).

In the Sean Connery film, *You Only Live Twice*, the terrorist organization known as SPECTRE is busy launching rockets from a dormant volcano in Japan and using them to kidnap both Russian and American satellites from orbit. SPECTRE's resentment of the reigning world powers here parallels that of the Titans in Hesiod's *Theogony*, in which the Titans are the resentful earth children sent by Mother Gaia to block Zeus from ascending to the top of Mount Olympus in order to consolidate his rule.

And, as is typical of so many pop culture narratives, the villains in the Bond stories often exhibit deformities which mark them unmistakably as members of the underworld powers: the mechanical hands, already mentioned, of Dr. No; Blofeld, the leader of SPECTRE, whose face in the celluloid version of *You Only Live Twice* is marred by a terrible gash; Hugo Drax, the one-eyed villain of Fleming's novel *Moonraker*; Scaramanga, the man with three nipples who is the villain of *The Man With the Golden Gun*; the asthmatic Le Chiffre in *Casino Royale*; or the weak heart of Mr. Big in Fleming's novel *Live and Let Die* which causes his black skin to take on a gray pallor. Such villains are close analogues of the Titans of Greek myth, or the Fomorians of Irish legend, or the *rakshasas* of Hindu theology, all of whom are invariably deformed in some way: one-armed, one-handed, multiple-armed, one-eyed, etc. This marks them as essentially chaotic beings inimical to the smooth functioning of the world order.

And that world order is the global stage upon which the Bond dramas are played out. Thus, the Bond universe of villains is a world of ancient mythic beings disguised as Cold War undesirables who have hi-jacked new technologies which they wish to put to ill uses. Bond's job as an ancient dragon-slaying hero recast as a Cold warrior is to make sure that the machines which have turned their users into villains by transforming them into mere servomechanisms do not get the upper hand.

And who can say, looking at today's world, run by bureaucratic and corporate powers which are forever attempting to intimidate and tyrannize over mere human individuals with their cold, impersonal systems of inhuman orderliness, that Bond has really been very successful?

Eighth Media Transformation:
The Celluloid Hero

Mad Max

Intake

Mad Max is entirely post-urban. Whereas, with Captain Nemo we had seen a complete hostility to civilization of any kind (to such a degree that Nemo refused ever to set foot on land), and with Tarzan there was an oscillation between the city and the jungle, although Tarzan much preferred the jungle and its less evolved apes as his companions. With Zorro, the superhero was captured into the orbit of a pueblo-style proto-Los Angeles to become part of its immune system, just as Sam Spade, meanwhile, in San Francisco was already functioning as the immune system of that city, for it was his job to keep the Titans and Fomorians out of it. Conan's hostility to cities was thorough, but not so thorough that we didn't occasionally find him in the role of a king, as in the very first Conan tale, "The Phoenix on the Sword" or in the later Conan novel *The Hour of the Dragon*. And with the comic book superheroes, we saw a full-fledged functioning immune system at work in the city of New York.

But with the Mad Max films, civilization is now a thing of the past. Max Rockatansky has come unplugged from all cities and become a rogue element, a loner who drifts through the waste land in search of, precisely, Nothing. He has no goals and sees no Vision. What befalls him is whatever situation he just happens to be thrust in at the moment. A postmodern hero, in other words.

The original trilogy, though, does have an arc that tells a story, namely how a celluloid hero who comes unplugged from civilization and who is a contemporary equivalent of the ancient dying and reviving god (specifically embodying the powers of the snake to shed its skin: Max is "killed" in each film and then revived, as it were) is slowly transformed into the savior of civilization, growing wings in the process. Max moves from slithering on the ground like a snake, to a transformation in which the serpent grows wings like Qetzalcoatl and ascends into the heavens.

In the first film *Mad Max* (1979), Max is a police officer, although of a special type, the Main Force Police, which governs the roads. He is immediately connected, therefore, to the dromosphere, which it is his job to govern and control. Indeed, whereas the opening shot of the typical Western in its high period was always of the sky, Mad Max opens with a shot of the highway stretching like a black ribbon out across the infinitely smooth space of the Australian outback. Max's job as a cop is to act as an "Interceptor," or force of obstruction for stepping down the speeds of the dromosphere, that realm of speed which the conveyance of all vehicles constitutes (and named as such by Paul Virilio).[39] As Michel Foucault remarks, the police in the sixteenth century came into being precisely to regulate the flow of goods and services as the newly emerging bourgeoisie channeled them across roads, canals and rivers.[40] The police are a force of obstruction for stepping down the speeds of the dromospheric activity that takes place out beyond the walls of the city and begins to approach it with incoming commerce (or else sieges), in the flow of camels, donkeys, horses, chariots, and most recently, automobiles.

Civilization, in the first film, is crumbling, but it has not yet collapsed completely. The roads, however, are terrorized by an external proletariat in the form of motorcycle gangs–and in this respect, the film hybridizes the classic Western with the 1953 classic *The Wild One* (Max's leather outfit refers to Brando's)–a gang led by a villain known as Toecutter (who survives, almost miraculously, into the 2015 sequel *Mad Max 4: Fury Road*). When Max, at the start of the film, chases one of their gang off the road–a man named Night Rider–Max becomes marked for death. The motorcycle gang avenge the death of Night Rider by killing Max's best friend "Goose" and then they run down his wife and infant child on the highway.

This is the first "death" of Max in the trilogy, for he responds by shedding the skin of his former identity as a cop and goes rogue, exchanging his yellow and blue police car for a souped-up version known as the "last of the V8 Interceptors," a slick black hot rod that he uses to track down and overpower the villains (all except their leader Toecutter). He is, however, emotionally numbed by the film's conclusion, and drives off into the outback to an uncertain destination. The city as environment for the Hero as immune cell is now but a memory.

Compression

In *The Road Warrior* (1981), which resumes perhaps ten years later (and takes place, chronologically, after *Fury Road*), Max is still driving a worn down version of the very same V8 Interceptor, and he is now living only for one thing: the gasoline that will power his car across the smooth spaces of the endless waste land. Early on in the film, he meets the so-called "Gyro captain," a man who pilots a single-unit gyrocopter and with whom he forms a reluctant partnership. The Gyro captain represents a mechanized version of the powers of the bird, just as

Max, with his constant deaths and resurrections (or what the theoretician Catherine Malabou would call "destructive plasticity")[41] incarnates the power of the snake to shed its skin, time after time. Max and the Gyro captain must combine forces, bird *and* snake, to help deliver a besieged group of nomads who are living in a temporary encampment surrounded by rubber tires, where they have managed to create their own fuel. They have formed a fortress around the pumpjack and are storing its fuel inside of a tanker, but do not have the rig to drive the tanker. Thus, the fortress becomes what theoretician Paul Virilio terms a weapon of obstruction–i.e. ditches, ramparts, bastions–against dromospheric weapons of destruction–i.e. lances, bows, cannons, missiles.[42] It is an ancient conflict, as old as the first cities, compressed and miniaturized by the film's director George Miller for mass consumption.

Hence, Max's job: he must fetch a rig that he had seen out on the highway in exchange for getting his car back and more fuel, the only thing he cares about anymore. When the job is done, and he attempts to leave the nomadic encampment, however, the barbarians of the waste land nearly kill him: they shoot his dog and blow up his beloved V8 Interceptor (this is his second "death"). Upon his resurrection–for the serpent god cannot be killed but only temporarily–he agrees to drive the rig and haul the tanker across the highway as a decoy while the rest of the nomads of the "encampment" drive north to new horizons. Thus, in the second film, driving vehicles is Max's *only* function. He refuses to take any paternal responsibilities for a young feral boy with a boomerang who stows away on the truck, insisting on Max as the Lord of the Dromosphere to become his "father."

Ignition

Everything that had been inceptual in the second film grows, magnifies and expands in the third film of the original trilogy, *Mad Max: Beyond Thunderdome* (1985). There is some devolution to be sure: the V8 Interceptor is gone, and at the film's opening Max has been reduced to riding in a vehicle pulled not by his beloved gasoline but by a chain of camels. However, the Gyro captain's tiny one man gyrocopter has in the intervening years magnified into a small airplane, which, at the film's opening, he and his ten year old son pilot by hi-jacking Max's caravan and riding it to the nearest market village, a place called Barter Town, a sort of primitive Viking-like trading post with aspirations of becoming a city. Max traverses the desert on foot to go there because he wants his camels back. Motion across the smooth spaces of the desert has become his only *raison d'etre*. He must be kept in motion at all times, at all costs.

Barter Town, however, is now operating on the axial plane of organization: whereas *The Road Warrior* had been one vast gigantic smooth space across which nomads could slide, completely deterritorialized on an entirely horizontal surface–Barter Town is a vertical structure which trades out *The Road Warrior*'s horizontality for a stratified axis. It is organized, in the manner of all ancient cosmic cartographies, in three strata: that is to say, it has a middle world or mesocosm where the merchants do their business, but it also has an upper world of the aristocracy ruled by a matriarch named "Auntie," who is perpetually at war with the denizens of the city's underworld, a place where pigs are used to generate the methane that powers the city's electricity. Max, who has come unplugged from all city structures and is antipathetic to them all, finds himself caught in between this difference engine of conflict between the Powers Below and the Powers Above: he is tasked with descending downward to pick a fight with Master-Blaster, a giant who carries a dwarf on his shoulders, a dwarf who happens to be the only man who understands the formulae for creating the machines that power the city's electricity. He is forever undermining Auntie's authority by shutting off the electricity with periodic embargoes, and she wants his body guard, Blaster, dead. It is the ancient war of the aristocracy against the priesthood, or in this case, the priest of the machines.

The dispute must be settled within a domical structure known as Thunderdome, a neo-Medieval restructuring of a gladiatorial arena, or what Heiner Muhlmann would call a space set aside within the city-as-zone-of-cooperation for a zone of maximal stress.[43] The results of the battle against Master-Blaster involves the death of the giant, but his braniac Master, the dwarf, survives. And Max, once again–this time for his refusal to kill the giant himself (Auntie's Praetorian guard does it for him)– must endure yet another death (his third in the series): exile into the desert, to die of thirst among the dunes.

But he is resurrected this time by a tribe of feral children (hence, the single feral child with the boomerang of *The Road Warrior* has, in the third film, expanded and multiplied into an entire tribe). Since he has refused to play the paternal role for the feral child, now he is forced to play Father to *an entire tribe* of children. Be careful what task you refuse: it may come back upon you tenfold.

This time, he is resurrected by the children, who nurse him back to health after his ordeal in the sand dune desert. They tell him that he is the awaited Messiah, a man named Captain Walker who, their tale goes, piloted the 747 that crashed into the desert and from which, somehow, the children have descended from the survivors. The petroglyphic image they show him looks exactly like him: Max with leather jacket and gray winged hair, with arms spread wide like he is flying, and all the little children lined up in rows on his arms. Indeed, they even place an airline pilot's cap on his head which they have adorned with the wings of a bird.

When they take him out to the desert to show him the immense ruins of the crashed 747, we realize that the Gyro Captain's single seat helicopter, which had grown at the opening of the third film into a small airplane, has now grown further as a signifier into a dinosauric flying apparatus. But it is an apparatus that no longer belongs to the Gryo Captain, for the children, in their mythology, have specifically (re)assigned it to Max. They want him, in other words, to transform from a snake into a gigantic bird who will carry them all on his back to Tomorrowmorrow-land, that is to say, to the ruins of the great cities. They want him to become a mythical savior being–one who, like Prometheus or Romulus, becomes a founder of civilizations by teaching their inhabitants the various arts and crafts. He demurs, of course, but they refuse to see him in any other role.

Thus, Max's persona in this film shifts not only from that of serpent to bird, but from the Lord of the Highways to the Lord of the Airways. When he finally does lead the children back to Barter Town, from which they escape aboard a tiny train, the Gyro captain's services are called upon once again, and Max insists that he fly the children away to wherever they want to go. The plane is too heavy to bear Max's weight along with all the children, but he agrees to sacrifice himself on their behalf and drives a truck that crashes into the opposing forces of Auntie's Praetorian Guard from Barter Town who want their dwarf, with all his equations, returned to them.

So, in a sense, the film does end with Max transforming into a bird and carrying the children on his back, flying them away like Garuda out of ancient Indian myth, back to the ruins of the cities, which they intend to repopulate and light back up again.

Exhaust

Thus, Max as the figure who had come unplugged from the city-as-apparatus-of-capture, ends by effectuating the means of its reanimation. He shifts from playing the role of outcaste to that of Founding God of Civilization, like Osiris or Cain.

But the film's final image of campfires burning in the windows of the abandoned skyscrapers of Sydney suggests the possibility of a new civilization *without* a dromosphere. A civilization in which the internal combustion engine, with its four-stroke cycle, simply no longer exists, and where roads no longer function to convey anything but faded markers of a previous age, like the ruins of Roman roads in modern Britain. Roads of transport, that is, must shift to become neuronal highways that light up new pathways in the brain whereby new Visions of sustainable societies may emerge. Cars must give way to neurotransmitters as the task of Saint Christopher, patron of roads, is handed over to Gabriel, the angel who presides over communications.

Hence, the irony of Max as god of the highways becoming the civilizational founder of a society *without roads*. And perhaps it is a telling fact that the sequel to the trilogy, *Mad Max 4: Fury Road* (2015) is not so much a sequel that occurs chronologically *after* the trilogy but in between the first and second films.

Back in the days before the transformation, in other words, when he was still the patron god of roads and highways.

Ninth Media Transformation: Television

The X-Files

Dyad

By now, Mulder and Scully have become almost as famous as their literary prototypes Holmes and Watson. Indeed, in many ways, they strongly resemble this earlier pair of detectives who stand at the threshold of the birth of the forensic genre. Watson, like Scully, was also trained as a medical doctor, and Holmes, like Mulder, was the man of genius for whom solutions to any given mystery would come in a flash of intuition like a revelation from the gods, leaving a bewildered Watson struggling to keep up. But unlike Watson, Scully normally offers an alternative explanation for the given mystery, one that, she typically boasts, is based upon a scientific and rational view of the world. In this respect, she resembles Holmes rather more than Watson, for Holmes was bent upon sterilizing the grimy streets of Victorian London of its human bacterial infections of irrationalism and emotionalism, whereas Mulder applies his intellect to the task of bringing demons and devils, rather than bacteria, into focus.

And therein lies the basic–and rather obvious–tension between the protagonists of *The X-Files* that gave the show its momentum, for the conflict between science and spirituality is one of the primary reasons why the show attracted so many viewers. Of course, it is on the side of spirituality that the show's creator Chris Carter weighs in, for *The X-Files* is all about how the hypertrophic development of science has unduly restricted the purview of modern Western man, causing him to exclude the realm of the paranormal from serious consideration. Detractors of the show will wave their hand at this sort of thing and dismiss it as the product of New Agey California kitsch, but Carter's vision is an important and, I think, accurate assessment of the sorts of conflicts that are currently struggling within the two souls of Western man.

Since about the middle of the nineteenth century, our society has been undergoing a metamorphosis, brought on largely by the effects of its own technological evolution. The development of electric media—telegraph, telephone, radio, cinema, television—have accelerated the metabolism of the culture to light speed and this has resulted in the meltdown of both literacy and Newtonian science while a new kind of spatio-temporal awareness, much more akin to the spatio-temporal awareness of tribal man, has come to replace the old visual bias upon which rationalism and three dimensional space alike are predicated. The acceleration of culture to light speed, in other words, has flattened out our world into an aperspectival wilderness populated by two-dimensional beings out of ancient myth and the masked apparitions of tribal man.

The end result of this shift has been to open up the floodgates of Western man's repressions, and to unleash an avalanche of demons, devils and astral spirits, which are now loose and flitting about, looking for warm skulls within which to build their nests.

The X-Files is merely a documentation of this process.

Word vs. Icon

While it is true that the show's protagonists, Mulder and Scully, largely embody the opposed points of view of science and the paranormal, this simple dichotomy is a *bit* more complicated by the fact of Scully's Catholicism. To Mulder, organized religion is a put-on for the gullible and so this puts *him* in the role of the skeptic vis a vis Scully, who is a genuine believer in her own faith. Thus, the opposition commonly formulated between Scully and Mulder as that of science vs. superstition ought really to be reformulated as that between organized institutions (for both science and religion are highly organized and bureaucratic) vs. maverick eclecticism. Scully has a faith in authority that Mulder does not share, and it takes a long time for her to become convinced that the government she works for cannot be trusted.

It is worth pausing for a moment to consider the implications of Scully's background as a Catholic for her role in the show. Catholicism may be classified as an iconophilic religion, one that–like Hinduism–relies heavily for the communication of its ideas upon pictorial imagery. And when one considers that most of the imagery which haunts the Catholic imagination is brutal and violent, with punctured, bleeding representations of Christ, and twisted and torn saints, one wonders to what degree growing up around such imagery may have prepared Scully to accept that badly damaged bodies are an everyday occurrence. As a medical doctor, she is forever carving up dead bodies in autopsies for which Mulder eagerly awaits proof of his, to her, rather bizarre theories. Perhaps, then, Scully's childhood exposure to the Catholic imagery of sadism and torture prepared her to accept that such mangled corpses are "normal" and therefore do not require exotic or bizarre explanations for how they got that way.

In addition, such an upbringing may help to explain her lack of interest in metaphysical explanations of the world like those which preoccupy Mulder, for her religion has already given her ready made answers for such complex cosmological issues as the origin and destiny of the universe, the intervention of the divine in the form of angels (rather than extraterrestrials), and so forth. She has no more interest in occult or paranormal explanations for such phenomena than had Marshall McLuhan, who was also a practicing Catholic with little interest in mythology, the occult or the paranormal. His main concerns were the same as Scully's: science, technology and the media.

If Scully's Catholic background helps to explain her skepticism regarding Mulder's theorizing, it is possible that Mulder's Jewish background sheds some light on *his* particular orientation to the world (although Mulder, unlike Scully, is lapsed). For Judaism is as iconophobic as Catholicism is iconophilic. In Mulder's past, then, there would have been no imagistic preparation in his subconscious for accepting all these twisted and torn bodies as in any way "normal." Lacking such a background, they seem anything *but* normal to him, so he goes in quest of other explanations than those which are obvious to the eye, explanations which are part of larger, grander plans for the working out of time and history. Mulder's quest leads him into an apocalyptic vision of aliens about to invade the earth and wipe out all human life, and a cosmogony that begins with the aliens present on the planet *before* the advent of human beings. "In the beginning was the Word," is how the Old Testament puts it, for the Word is the Logos, which means a pattern or structure, and implies a master plan in accordance with which all things are shaped. Mulder is searching for a means of making Time into a linear, connected story, just as the Jews interpreted everything that happened to them as part of a larger narrative with a beginning, a middle and an end. The Old Testament is really one big novel with the Jews themselves cast as protagonist. It is a linear, connected vision of history that is the product of an alphabetically minded people with a strong written, exegetical tradition.

To everyone else around him, however, including Scully, Mulder is a paranoid. He is forever suspecting his supervisors and colleagues in the F.B.I. of withholding, and covering up, evidence that might prove the existence of extraterrestrials. But in fact, he is really a metanoid (from *metanoia*, meaning "conversion, or change in one's beliefs") who is sifting through the detritus of the past, with all its sloughed off spiritual environments, looking through a rubbish heap of broken dreams, archaic theories, and myths for the One Vision that will make sense out of the chaos of modernity. He is questing for the Great Myth that will eliminate the cognitive dissonance at the root of all our paranoia and bring about a metanoiac shift in our civilization from one mental bandwidth to the next.

Eye / Ear

If it is true, as McLuhan pointed out, that electric culture has exteriorized everything that Western man has repressed since the Renaissance, then Mulder is the cathode ray hero who is the very conduit of this electric reversal, dedicated to putting back into the center of waking consciousness the monsters and demons repressed for the past five hundred years. For the moment in which this repression took place can be pointed to symbolically in the work of Hieronymous Bosch who, right around the year 1500, collected all the goblins and gargoyles from the walls of Medieval cathedrals and dumped them into the new three dimensional spaces of his paintings. It was at that moment that the monsters disappeared, as it were, through a crack in the earth that then sealed itself up for five centuries. (In the episode known as "Signs and Wonders," Mulder and Scully, significantly, encounter one of Bosch's paintings hanging on the wall of a snake cult's church).

Bosch's gallery of demons did not fully resurface in our culture until Forrest J. Ackerman in the late 1950s established a fan magazine known as *Famous Monsters of Filmland*, upon every cover of which some monster out of the previous three or four decades of horror films was represented in lurid oil paint. To ponder a panorama of back issues of this magazine, all lined up on a single page, is to gaze at Bosch's monsters resurfaced anew *inside* of electronic culture. And it is precisely such a galley provisioned with monsters that *The X-Files* as a 1990s television show drew upon for its reserves.

Mulder's role in *The X-Files* is to act as a sort of medium for conducting the demons and devils of mythic, and especially tribal man, back into our culture. And since tribal man is also oral man, in the sense that his knowledge is patterned into orally told tales which must be kept in existence through the simple act of recitation, it is no exaggeration to say that tribal man is also *ear* man, for his entire world view is based upon acoustics. Hence, in *Finnegans Wake*, the name of the central character, Humphrey Chimpden *Ear*wicker, whose initials stand for H.C.E., or "Here Comes Everybody," is Joyce's way of demonstrating that in electric society, Western man has traded an eye for an ear, and that it is now the ear which is the central organ of symbolic significance.

Mulder, then, is the man of the *ear*, whose head is perpetually cocked, listening for the scuttling sounds of one or another creature hiding in the shadows, while Scully, who is forever opening up corpses to see what is inside them, is attuned to the *eye* (notice that she wears glasses, whereas Mulder does not). Scully's world is that of western science, a world built around the eye as its center of focus, a world of dissected corpses, Vesalian woodcuts, Cartesian grids, Rembrandt's anatomy lessons, and the erection of a mechanical view of the universe as a series of moving parts. The study of the physical body alone, upon which the image of the universe in western physics was based, led to the exclusion of the etheric body which animates it as well as to the exclusion of the *anima mundi* which, up until that time, had been the indwelling soul animating the planets. All of these scientific achievements were inspired by the idea of a corpse, which is incapable of any movement beyond the pushings and pullings of its limbs during an autopsy. Thus, this intensely visual world led to the triumph of mechanism, capitalism and three dimensional visual space as a container within which objects rested. It is also a world in which the role of sound is muted, for once the music of the spheres had been shut off, Pascal was inspired to say: "The silence of these eternal spaces terrifies me."

If you want to *see* into the interior of something you have to cut it open and turn it inside out. Sound, on the other hand, is a sense that is used to fathom the interior of something. If you want to know whether a wall is hollow or not, you bang on it. Mulder is attempting to restore the ancient world of *sound*, of acoustic phenomena associated with tribal man and his masked apparitions.

To clarify this, consider as a contrast to the Western development of the sense of sight, the world created by India. Here we find a society in which the eyes are *closed*, a world in which a philosophy of sound vibration builds up an entire cosmology based upon acoustic resonance, of mantras and chants, of prayers and oral recitations of sacred texts. Writing came late to India, and even then, most sacred texts were not immediately written down, but held in the memory and passed along orally. And these are incredibly intricate texts, so India's feat of memorization and oral transmission was a prodigious one. The explora-

185

tion of the physical body in India began with yoga, in which the eyes are closed and through deep breathing techniques the inner world is *sounded*. Hence, by unplugging, as it were, the sense of sight, and plugging in that of hearing, the Hindus were led to the discovery of a complex cosmology of a chain of supernatural beings which inhabited the universe on its *inside*. Hence, all the *asuras, rakshasas, danavas, gandharvas, apsarases, yakshas, kinnaras, nagas,* etc, which compose the Indian chain of being from Brahmaloka at the top of the universe to Naraka at the bottom, is a world discovered through the closing of the eyes and *listening*. (Indeed, the *rishis* were said not to have composed the *vedas*, but to have *heard* them).

This is precisely the world that Mulder is attempting to revive within the West by banging his hand against the walls of the cosmos in order to awaken its interior devils and demons, asleep since the Renaissance. So *The X-Files*, from this point of view, is an interior reawakening, through Mulder's sonic applications, of the world of tribal man and his mythic chains of beings running through the cosmos which our Western amplification of the sense of sight at the expense of all other senses forced it to exclude from consideration.

Chain of Being

All of this may seem as though we have taken a left turn into madness. And in a sense, we have, for in madness lies the very demons and astral spirits which kidnap the soul and make off with it, and that is precisely what *The X-Files* is all about.

The various monsters, beasts and goblins of *The X-Files* are a retrieval of an ancient cosmology, common to all the high civilizations, of a great chain of being of astral spirits. In the Christian tradition as epitomized for us by Pseudo-Dionysius the Areopagite in his *Celestial Hierarchy*, we find these beings laid out into a hierarchy of angels descending from the most sublime at the top–Seraphim, Cherubim and Thrones–to those progressively further away from God and closer to earth–Powers, Virtues, Dominions, and finally to Angels, Archangels and Principalities. In the imagination of nineteenth century esoteric societies, this cosmology was revived by the German mystic Rudolf Steiner in his vision of elemental spirits inhabiting the various rocks and stones and waters of the earth at one end, while a complex hierarchy of angelic beings mounted up toward the heavens at the other. Unlike the traditional Christian hierarchy, however, all these beings were involved in a process of spiritual evolution, the beings of one level striving to rise up in the course of time to occupy the level immediately above, in good nineteenth century evolutionary fashion.

Such a chain of beings exists also in *The X-Files*, but one must watch a great number of the show's episodes to become aware of this. The hierarchy is not formally and consciously organized by the show's creators, and in this respect the show differs from that of the tradition, but the hierarchy is there nonetheless, evident to the discerning eye.

The leading theme of the show is the invasion of the human being by occult entities, both astral (i.e. of the soul) and physical (of the immune system). For the mind has an immune system, too, which is a normal and logical extension of the body's and if it is not strong enough to defend itself against attack, then it will be abducted by one or another of the various creatures which appear on the show in order to make off with it.

According to traditional esoteric theory (going clear back to the Egyptians), the human being is not just comprised of a simplistic body and soul, but is a sort of nest of Chinese boxes of subtle bodies, each one more refined and complex than the one below it, in imitation of the heavenly hierarchies, which grow more refined the further they ascend. In the parlance of Rudolf Steiner (which I use here not because I am an Anthroposophist, but simply because it is ready to hand) the physical body is the lowest, something that all animate beings share in common with the world of rocks and minerals. But in the next level up, the human being also possesses an etheric body, the motivating principle of all animate life. It is the presence of an etheric body which makes plants plants and not rocks. Likewise, in humans, the etheric body maintains and organizes the physical body and also repairs it when it falls sick (especially during sleep). The etheric body also includes the function of memory, in a mysterious way. In the next level up, human beings possess an astral body, which is what they share in common with all animals. This is simply waking consciousness and it is what differentiates animals from plants. But humans, in addition, also have a mental body which animals do not have, and this is yet another complex series of nested functions which we need not get into here, for we have sketched enough of Steiner's view to make it clear that there are four main bodies: physical, etheric, astral and mental.

Now, the monsters that we meet in *The X-Files* are not just random, for each of them preys upon one or another of man's subtle bodies. Many of the most memorable, in fact, prey upon the physical body. In the episode known as "Squeeze," for example, a man with an elastic body named Eugene Victor Tooms is really a creature who must hibernate every 30 years, but he can only do this after killing five people and eating their livers. In "2Shy," we encounter a serial killer who meets overweight women online and must eat their fatty tissue because of some genetic anomaly. In "Hungry," a fast-food restaurant employee kills people and sucks their brains out through a small hole in their heads. In "Teliko," an African man who is slowly losing his melanin can only survive by preying upon other black males and stripping the melanin from their skins, turning them ash white in the process.

The extraterrestrials which concern so much of the show's main "mythology," seem to be preoccupied with the etheric body, for they often tamper with both the human immune system as well as the memory. Abductees who have returned with microchips implanted into the backs of their necks will develop cancer if they attempt to remove the chips. Eventually, the aliens plan on colonizing the earth after they unleash a black virus plague that will wipe out all of humanity. Also, one of the common experiences of an abductee is a sense of "lost time" in which certain lacunae cannot be filled in with memory. The aliens frequently erase their victim's memories as a routine part of their operations.

Then there are those episodes in which certain beings prey upon the astral body. In the show called "Via Negativa," a cult leader who has the ability to project himself into the dreams of his worshippers, in which he appears floating in yoga posture with a third eye upon his forehead, kills his dreaming victims by crushing their skulls with an axe (that is to say, a thunderbolt, just as in Indian mythology, the god Shiva fires bolts of thunder from his middle eye, for axes and tridents have traditionally been symbolic of the thunderbolt of the monster-slaying warrior hero); in "Tithonus," a crime scene photographer who is somehow always first on the scene when a person has died (for he has premonitions of their deaths) photographs them in an attempt to catch a glimpse of Death making off with their astral bodies, for he himself is over one hundred and fifty years old and seems to be incapable of dying. In "Sleepless," a military experiment conducted during Vietnam involving the creation of soldiers who never need to sleep by performing brain surgery on them has resulted in the production of a man named the Preacher, who hasn't slept in 24 years, and who has developed the ability to project his waking dreams into 3D holograms of aggression which result in killing off the other sleepless soldiers who were part of the experiment. In "Avatar," Agent Skinner is preyed upon by a succubus who causes him to think he is murdering women, and so forth.

At the mental level, there are the mind parasites which feed off of human confusion, like the doll in Stephen King's episode "Chinga," which causes people to kill and maim themselves. In "Pusher," a serial killer is able to get people to do what he wants, since the presence of a brain tumor has given him special powers, including the ability to convince people to kill themselves in inventive ways. In "Wetwired," people become paranoid as a result of a hidden signal that is beamed to them through their television sets, and in a similar episode called "Blood," Mulder and Scully discover that a group of people who go on killing sprees are driven to do this as a result of poisoning by an experimental insecticide, LSDM, with properties similar to LSD, which causes them to hallucinate that electronic devices are telling them to kill people.

Thus, the creatures of the show are ultimately ancient monsters–like the various succubi, vampires, and ghouls distributed liberally throughout the episodes–which have been preying upon one or another of man's subtle bodies throughout the millennia, and for which special measures must be taken in order to insure that one's psychological and biological immune system is strong enough to resist such beings (for example, in the episode called "Millenium" we find out that one can protect oneself against zombies by standing in the middle of a circle made out of salt). But the show makes clear that the overarching vision of such predation is one of a vast immunological breakdown that is taking place in our society on a mass scale. *The X-Files* suggests that we are suffering from this mental and biological breakdown as a result of the weakening of our immune systems by techno-chemical oversaturation. On a daily basis, we are unwittingly soaking our bodies in radiation and chemicals: exposure to ELF fields from computer monitors, cell phones and radio and TV towers; EMF's radiated by powerlines, substations and transformers; carcinogenic chemicals like PCB's, PBDE's (found in flame retardants and known to interfere with thyroid function and neurological development); dioxins from paper mills, chemical plants and incinerators; bizarre chemicals known to cause reproductive system abnormalities in animals like phthalates (found in fragrant shampoos) and Bisphenol A (found in plastics); prefluorinated acids found in nonstick and stain-resistant coatings and known to cause birth defects and liver damage in lab animals; mercury-soaked fish; and the list goes on. Taken in isolation or small doses, these toxins might be innocuous enough, but in the kinds of daily chemical baths within which we immerse ourselves, it all adds up to a weakening of both mind and body. A weakening that makes it easier for malign spirits to take advantage of the body's lowered defenses.

The writers of *The X-Files* are attuned to these happenings, albeit subliminally, for such happenings float through the ether like radio waves where they are picked up by sensitive writers whose minds download them into the imagery of science fiction. Hence, viruses and bacteria appear magnified through the distorting lens of television as evil spirits invading the body. Disease turns up transformed into the strange, Kafkaesque vision of episodes like "S.R. 819" in which Agent Skinner is infected by microscopic nanotech machines which slowly destroy his body by making it as rigid as an exoskeleton.

Taken as a whole, these episodes all add up to a frankly pessimistic commentary about the state of the present health of

Western man, for such a vision of spiritual predation is akin to a nightmare in which shadowy entities creep into one's bedroom at night in order to kidnap one's astral body and make off with it. Sometimes, these dreams are mistaken for reality and said to be the result of extraterrestrial encounter and abduction, with attendant physical phenomena, such as micro implants and scars held up as "proof." But as the phenomenon of stigmata proves, what the mind imagines or fears can indeed materialize itself in the body.

If *The X-Files* is pessimistic about the current state of Western man's mental and physical health, it is even more bleak about where he is headed, as a consideration of the show's overarching "mythology" reveals.

The Mythology

Television is a medium that confers a certain elasticity upon narrative forms, stretching them across the space of many seasons and years until the story threads begin to exhibit signs of fraying. Consequently, in considering the overarching "mythology" (which in older written narratives would be known simply as the "frame") or plot that provides *The X-Files* with its narrative continuity over nine seasons, it is impossible to give a tidy summing up. However, the show's plot becomes increasingly coherent, and less ambiguous, as the seasons unfold, and so, in extremely compressed form, its narrative runs something like this:

Fox Mulder's sister was abducted, apparently by aliens, when he was seven years old. The desire to solve this mystery is what motivates him to hunt down, and prove, the existence of extraterrestrials, despite the scorn and resistance put up by the very government organization for which he works. He is convinced that the U.S. government knows that the aliens are real, but has lied about this to the American people and covered it up.

In the early episodes, we are never quite sure whether the aliens are real or invented by the government as a smokescreen, for we only catch furtive glimpses of their disappearing ships or hidden caches of their dead bodies which mysteriously disappear. It is possible, and at one point Mulder becomes certain, that the aliens are indeed a cover up invented by the government to disguise a more disturbing project involving experiments in human cloning and genetic engineering.

At one point, Scully herself is abducted, but when she returns, she has only hazy memories of her experience. Later, we learn that she had had genetic material extracted from her during the abduction, material that was used for the purpose of creating a child as a synthetic hybrid of human and extraterrestrial DNA. Scully discovers that a tiny microchip has been implanted in the back of her neck, and when it is removed, she contracts a form of nasal-pharyngeal cancer.

The show's primary villain is a mysterious figure known only as the Cigarette Smoking Man, for he is never seen without a cigarette for very long. He is an older man, apparently a high level government employee, and always seems to be behind the attempts to destroy any evidence that would confirm the existence of extraterrestrials. But he happens to have in his possession the cure for Scully's cancer, and at one point, several seasons in, he cuts a deal with Mulder and Scully's boss, Agent Skinner–whose loyalties are always divided between the X-Files and the shadowy higher ups from whom he takes his orders–to produce the cure in exchange for Skinner's doing a favor for him. Skinner agrees. Later, the favor turns out to involve the covering up of an episode in which a swarm of deadly bees gets loose and stings a few people to death. The bees are a central part of the show's iconography, for they are genetically engineered to carry a strange alien virus with which the government is planning to infect the population. Cigarette Man, however, produces the cure for Scully's cancer, another microchip, which is then reimplanted at the base of her skull, and her cancer vanishes.

In later seasons, as the mythology clarifies itself, we begin to learn what all this has been about. There is a war going on between two races of alien beings (for midway through the fifth season, the show's creators decide to make the ontological commitment to the reality of the aliens). One race has plans to invade and colonize the planet. The other, however, is a resistance force which does not agree with this idea (we are never told why). An internal, and high level group of government conspirators known as the Syndicate–which includes the Cigarette Man–has indeed been attempting to cover up their involvement with the colonizing race of aliens ever since Roswell, for they have been conducting a series of genetic experiments upon human abductees in order to create a race of alien-human hybrids to be used as slave labor for the colonizers when they arrive. The colonizers, whom we never see clearly, except only in quick glimpses, have black blood, and with this blood, they are planning upon spreading a viral plague in order to wipe out the human population prior to their arrival. The Syndicate has agreed to help spread this plague using their genetically engineered bees. The alien-human hybrids, as well as the rebel aliens, have green blood, but otherwise look human, although the rebels are shape-shifters who sometimes sew up all the orifices of their faces to prevent their being infected by the black virus. The rebels have committed themselves to hunting down and destroying all the alien-human hybrids, one by one, most of whom, however, are sickly anyway. While cooperating with the colonizers all along, however, the Syndicate changes its mind and begins to develop a vaccine against the "black oil" that will render them immune from the plague. But the rebel aliens manage to lure all the members of the Syndicate, together with their families, into a trap—with the exception of Cigarette Man—and murder them. It is uncertain whether the colonization will proceed or not.

The show, then, becomes more apocalyptic as it goes along. There is a pessimism evident here regarding the human relationship to the spirit world, for that is what aliens and extraterrestrials in popular imagery always signify: they are the gods of old returned anew in the vestments of science fiction cosmology. This is confirmed by the aliens' intention to use humanity as a slave labor force, for this is a cryptic allusion to the Mesopotamian myth of the creation of human beings as slaves for the gods, who did not wish to work for a living anymore. So they brought humans into being, who then set promptly to work in order to build cities with magnificent temples that would act as gigantic hotels to invite the gods down from heaven to stay with them. In some variations of this myth, moreover, the humans are created using the blood of some of the lower gods, so they are a sort of hybrid of human-divine DNA.

But the spirit world as pictured in *The X-Files* is ominous and threatening. Humanity, the show says, is on the verge of being stricken with a divine invasion in the form of a viral epidemic that will wipe out most of the population. Such terrifying imagery is typical of apocalyptic epochs in which, for one or another reason, the human relationship to the gods has been knocked out of alignment. During the late Hellenistic age, for example, in which the first apocalyptic writings of the Hebrews appeared, the Jews were not allowed to worship their god in their own traditional manner, due to the prohibitions placed upon them by the Greek ruler Antiochus IV Epiphanes. In response, the Maccabean revolt broke out, and the Jews expelled the Greeks and took over Palestine to run it for themselves until the coming of the Romans. This is the period from which such apocalyptic texts as the Book of Daniel and 2 Esdras date.

In the present case, it is the development of a hypertrophic science and technology that has disturbed the axial human-god alignment and done so much damage to the functioning of the earth's ecosystems that it has caused the planet to come down with a fever. The crisis is such that it calls for divine intervention. The neglected gods, once associated with the shrines and dolmens of this forest, that hill, or yonder river, no longer receiving their proper due, are about to intervene in the human condition in a big way. With their diminished status, they are only visible to us now in science fictional form as races of battling extraterrestrials contending for possession of the human soul. But as *The X-Files* shows us, the human soul is suffering from an auto immune disorder that will not allow it to resist these spiritual kidnappings and hi-jackings which we term "abductions." Such abductions and invasions are the result of enraged divinities who are tired of pesky humans making a mess out of their planet, for the gods of ancient myth–and hence, the aliens–are the earth's immune system, and when they perceive a threat to its proper health and functioning, they will send in their white blood cells–or in this case, the Grays–to take care of the situation. If it takes a plague to work as an antihuman biotic to rid the earth of its fever, so be it.

According to *The X-Files*, then, we are headed for a disaster, unless we can reprioritize our priorities. We must come, one way or another, to a recognition of a real spiritual dimension that lies both within us as well as in the outer world around us, and take the time that is necessary to cultivate and care for that dimension. Otherwise, the human species does appear to be headed for the period of the earth's Sixth Extinction and may not make it through to the other side.

This, then, is Mulder's task: to descend into the electron bath of our television sets and to return to us, the viewers, with a message from the outer darkness.

Tenth Media Transformation: Cable Television

Breaking Bad

Walter White has a problem: the model that he has been following as the "imaginary signification" to shape his life by isn't working. He is an affable high school chemistry teacher whose wife and in-laws do not respect him. They regard him as an amusing and powerless individual whom life has passed by. And indeed, he is a spineless, castrated husband and father who, for the most part, does what his wife tells him to do. She possesses the Phallus. He has to get it back.

His little domestic microsphere, furthermore, is leaking: the necessary funds to create a capitalist flow to keep it afloat in the post-2008 economy aren't there. Indeed, his household is rapidly sinking to the level of Barbara Ehrenreich's lower middle class of the "nickel and dimed" who are in constant danger of capsizing into foreclosure.

What to do?

The problem, as Vince Gilligan–a former writer of *The X-Files*–sees it, is one of image dynamics: Walter must scrap his identity as a domesticated suburbanite–"break" the mold, that is to say–and trade it out for one that will scale up his image to one more suitable for repairing his damaged family microsphere. In doing so, he traces a line of flight out onto the plane of immanence—i.e. the desert, in this case—and plugs himself into an altogether different imaginary signification, that, namely, of a barbarian tribal warlord.

The desert produces nomads, for it is itself a plane largely unmarked by striated space. While Walter and his sidekick Jessie Pinkman are out cooking crystal meth in their RV in the desert, Walter *thinks* he is merely making a marketable product, when in fact, he is melting down his own image in the alchemical alembic and transforming it into something more formidable. (Note that the three colors of alchemy, black, white and red are present in the names of *Schwarz*, his previous business associate, Walter *White* and Jessie *Pink*man. The alchemical stages of *nigredo, albedo* and *rubedo* end with the production of the magical *lapis exilis*, or philosopher's stone, that turns lead into gold. Here it is the production of the crystal meth that turns ordinary chemicals into capitalist flows.) But the real alchemy, of course, is the process of his own transformation into a modern tribal chieftain, for the desert is the nomadological plane of the Bedouin, the Berber, the Hun, the Avar, etc.

This transformation consists essentially in a 90 degree rotation of his axis of orientation: from a (failed and spineless) vertical and arborescent axis as domestic family man, to a horizontal and nomadological axis as wanderer-amongst-the tribes. This is also tantamount, though, to an exchange of legal spheres, for the rational legal system of checks and balances does not work out on the desert plains, but rather the old tribal eye-for-an-eye juridical system of blood vendettas, a "legal" world that is totally at odds with checks and balances. Blood and the way that it flows—as Ibn Khaldun wrote in his *Muqadimmah*, in which the Bedouin is always connected by blood relatives to the ruling powers, whereas once the city as a structure is built, it ruptures the connective tissues of these bloodlines and so produces the decadence of civilized life—is the *only* concern of the nomad. If it is spilled, it must be redressed with further spillage.

And so, the alchemical transformation of Walter's Image into that of a barbarian tribal war lord of a Southwestern desert drug empire brings along with it certain structures that are completely incompatible with those of a family man living an arborescent life inside the striated spaces of a contemporary city. In direct proportion to the ever-increasing size and scale of his Image, his wife grows ever more and more terrified of him as his Shadow looms over their house, and soon engulfs it. This is not Walter White, high school teacher and family man, but Heisenberg— the name of a modern alchemist, known these days as "quantum physicists"—a shadowy and powerful drug lord who ruthlessly dispenses with anyone who gets in the way of his greed.

Image dynamics, apparently, are not a thing to be taken lightly.

But this transformation does enable Walter to create a *supplement*—in the Derridean sense—out of the money that is generated from his manufacture of crystal meth, and it is a supplement that, at first, solves the family's financial problems and prevents the leaking microsphere from collapsing. But soon, the supplement becomes a surplus, and eventually devolves into an example of Bataille's "accursed share," a surplus, namely, that becomes a manifestation of so much excess energy that it has to be gotten rid of at all costs lest its build-up destroys the system.

Walter's partner Jessie Pinkman, on the other hand, inhabits the nomadological plane of immanence which today's crumbling cities are generating on the *insides* of their public spaces: namely, urban gangs, drug dealers and roving human wolf packs. In the age of failed systems of transcendence, Pinkman is an example of the hapless individual who is forced to construct his own artificial transcendence through the instruments of expansion that link him as part to the Whole via the drugs: crystal meth, at first; then later, heroin. (For the priest, the equivalent instruments of expansion are wine and wafer). These drugs allow him to construct his own *Transcendenz*, albeit an ersatz one, in which he is able to induce ecstatic trance flights of the kind known to shamans since Time began. But the constant process of separating his astral from his physical body generates a dissipative by-product: his house becomes full of wandering human ghosts who have themselves, for various reasons, come unplugged from their microspheres and collective assemblages. Pinkman's house becomes a pure plane of immanence filled with the destratified who have traced erratic lines of flight out onto a plane of consistency that they can never return from.

Walter, meanwhile, through the course of the show's five seasons, oscillates back and forth between Pinkman's nomadological plane of immanence and his own ruptured domestic microsphere. While Pinkman is busy plugging himself into ecstatic *Transcendenz*, Walter is inadvertently *unplugging* himself from his own domestic microsphere. He gradually constructs a drug empire which becomes a sovereign overcoding of the Southwest with himself cast as barbarian warlord at the head of a violent war machine.

But his empire captures, traps and overcodes the tiny–and ever-tinier as the show goes on–domestic microsphere that he had built it in the first place to protect. It soon becomes apparent that the captured microsphere of the little house in Albuquerque is too small to accommodate his ever-expanding Image as barbarian warlord, and soon, he finds himself almost literally growing out of it like a giant, or like Alice once she has taken the pill from the table and finds herself too large to fit inside the house. When Walter turns back to speak to his family, they are like small, frightened children cowering at his feet: they are too terrified to recognize what he has become. The Image has swallowed him up.

As an immunological response, however, the metabolism of his domestic microsphere soon ejects him as a waste by-product of its dissipative functioning. The surplus that he has created actually *pushes* him onto the Outside of this microsphere, where he finds himself in exile along with the accursed share of his surplus millions, which are now useless. Vince Gilligan, the show's writer and creator, is an almost Kubrickean master of irony.

By the show's end, the transformation is complete: Walter White is now fully and thoroughly a nomad and can only live like Cain, a wanderer moving horizontally across all systems whatsoever. The domestic sphere, on the other hand, is by nature arborescent: today's suburbanites are the contemporary equivalent of farmers and villagers living in houses rooted to the spot (locked in by mortgages and bank loans) in their plant-like stasis.

Walter, though, is no longer a plant, but a spore, drifting across the countryside, too large and legendary, too full of myth and proverb now, to be domesticated any longer. He has, indeed, become a proverbial figure: the Wanderer With Millions He Couldn't Use. By the show's conclusion, we see him fading–like Tyrone Slothrop in Pynchon's novel *Gravity's Rainbow* –into the mists of myth and legend, a victim of inadvertent image dynamics that made him too large for daily life in the suburbs.

What to do?

When a man's identity has been scrapped, the standard response is to turn to violence as a quest for a new identity, as McLuhan pointed out, and so in the last episodes, Walter is preparing for the final act of violence that will redeem him.

As Flannery O'Connor said: "(Only) The Violent Bear it Away."

The Walking Dead

As I have pointed out elsewhere, television is now *the* great new medium that is taking over the role once occupied by cinema, especially the role of miniaturizing ancient and long forgotten cosmologies. Indeed, Frank Darabont's television show, *The Walking Dead*, based on a series of graphic novels, is one of the best of these new shows and I want to say a few words about it here.

The Walking Dead is a sort of experimental laboratory for probing utopian societies, and the evolution of the show thus far–currently in its third season–has progressed through a series of such miniaturized societies. In this respect, the show is continuing where the great utopian / dystopian narratives of classical literature, from Plato's *Republic* to Fritz Lang's *Metropolis* (and then onward into such celluloid narratives as *The Truman Show* and *Dark City*) left off. Film has currently traded the exploration of multiple utopias for precisely *one* utopia, that namely, of comic book Gotham, and has left the exploration of other utopic / dystopic possibilities for television.

The show's first season explored, and then rejected, the modern megalopolis as ideal society, finding it a corrupt world of the walking dead, an old, very old metaphor for the spiritually asleep and ignorant human being locked into the mode of forgetfulness of Being. The first season polarized the corrupt and decadent metropolis against the exospheric nomadic society, privileging the latter social formation as a stateless mode of wandering and exile in which experiments with new social structures no longer bound and constrained by the City as a pressurized apparatus of social capture were undertaken.

The second season moved from the city and the nomadic tribe to the farm as ideal society, capturing an Andrew Wyeth nostalgia for a primordial American way of life as idealistic. During the Industrial Revolution, populations in the West migrated from the countryside to the great new cities, but nowadays, the city is precisely the place to escape *from*. Hence, the subtext of John Carpenter's *Escape from New York* and also *The Truman Show*. Whereas in the time of the Black Death in the fourteenth century, the city, too, was infested with the dead (in that case, with those killed by the plague) and had to be escaped from into the countryside: hence the characters of Bocaccio or Chaucer who leave the city behind on their way to greener pastures. But now, once again, on the turn of the historical spiral, the city is infested with a new kind of dead, the walking dead, that is to say, consumers entranced into hypnotic states who have had their upper brain functions zeroed out by new technologies (not to mention pharmaceutical drugs) and consumer advertising that have turned them into zombies. The authentic life, that is to say, must be found elsewhere.

But the farm turns out to be merely an illusion of safety and is very quickly infested with the dead, just as nowadays there is no quiet place on earth left where one can be free of the noise of the beer-swilling, barbecue-grilling mob.

In the third season, the archetype of the prison as dystopia is polarized against the new utopia of the ideal American small town. Neither isolated farm nor crowded metropolis, the American small town is held up as a potential ideal, at least by contrast with the hell of the prison, but it, too, is found wanting. We are not told yet, but it is clear that the small town is merely the surface facade–like Smalltown America at the entrance to Disneyland–of a bizarre and sinister social experiment of manipulation and crowd control.

The prison which the wandering band of protagonists holes up in is, of course, a kind of updating of Dante's Hell: it is an Anti-Sphere, to use Peter Sloterdijk's term, not an ideal society at all, but a place where the social remainder, the supplemental *excess of those who do not fit in*, as it were, spills over.

When the protagonists, at the end of Season Three, make their way from the prison to the small town in order to rescue their abducted friends, we realize that the show is replicating Dante's ascent from Hell to Purgatory, for the small town is a kind of purgatory where one must remain stranded, like Andrea, until one's karmic debt is worked off.

Dante's Hell, though, was a foreshadowing of Foucault's Disciplinary Society, for it clearly prefigures the Great Confinement of the 17th century, in which the mad were for the first time gathered into asylums, an institution whose sequel was the advent of the prison at the end of the eighteenth century. Foucault is thus revealed as a kind of disguised science fiction writer who picked up from where Dante left off, for his retroactive portrait of the European institutions of discipline and confinement is a vision of Europe as a Hell to be escaped from, a dystopian place in which a hidden power elite manipulates the individual from behind the scenes, as it were. Dante's Hell *is* Foucault's prison, in which Foucault stands in for the reader as a sort of modern Virgil guiding him through the dark journey.

But the myth of the world as a giant prison is, of course, an old motif of Gnostic mythology, for the Gnostics, too, imagined that the world was a grand prison manipulated by a power elite known as the Archons, who constructed human bodies as material prisons for souls as fallen sparks of light. The world as a whole was imagined as a physical hell to be escaped from at any and all cost, precisely through the process of gnosis, or the remembrance through anamnesis of one's celestial origins in the Plenum of Light.

Those who had forgotten their soul's own origins in the realm of Light, however, were regarded as "sleepwalkers," or, in other words, the walking dead, cut off as they were from any remembrance of the Kingdom of Light.

The image of the zombie as a figure of devolved consciousness, in which the neocortex and the mammalian midbrain have been shut down, with the human individual reduced to operating merely at the state of the reptilian brain stem is an image of spiritual degeneration back to the motive economic concerns of a merely animalistic way of existence, a way of existence, of being *thrown*, as Heidegger would say, that is not at all a proper and efficient use of the human being's potential as Dasein.

The risen dead was an image, in Biblical times, of the Last Judgment: all the paintings of the Last Judgment, especially of the fifteenth century Netherlandish painters such as Rogier van der Weyden and Jan Van Eyck, show the dead rising from their graves as a sign of the End of History. The image of the risen, homeless dead, then, has actually been with us as a sort of hidden Western iconotype all along. Its present popularity, however, is linked with the fact that we have indeed, as Steven Spielberg pictured it for us in *Close Encounters of the Third Kind*, reached the End of History in which the realized utopian consumer paradise as the modern equivalent of the New Jerusalem has descended from the realm of metaphysics to become actualized on the plane of the real. The task of history has thus reached completion.

We can all rest now, and go home.

Or just become zombies, robbed of a historical eschaton, wandering without aim or place in the ruins of the capitalist mega-paradise at the End of History.

Epilogue

So, we have traversed a long course: we began with Captain Nemo, a larger than life character who came at us out of the smooth spaces of the ocean–that vast blue dromosphere--to announce the advent of the Giant Human who was, at least initially, hostile to the very idea of civilization itself. (Indeed, Nemo's *raison d'etre*, simply to exist in a state of constant motion across vast distances, is the same as Mad Max's–only in a post-civilizational mode–on the turn of the historical spiral decades later, across the smooth spaces of the desert).

With Tarzan, we saw the proto-superhero emerge by recapturing the Paleolithic hunter at the dawn of civilization, and also enfolding within him as a signifier the myth of human evolution from apes protected by the eternal canopy of trees to the urban, language-speaking dweller of the modern cosmopolis. Tarzan is inimical to the city as such, but retrieves the hero as Paleolithic hunter: that is to say, a being capable of great deeds like bringing down mammoths or fighting cave bears. But with Zorro, the superhero became caught and captured into the orbit of the Proto-city, an early draft of Los Angeles as a Mexican farming village with no higher aspirations than those of the mud brick villages of the ancient Neolithic, that is to say, to till the soils and plough the furrows across the generations in an essentially a-historic mode. It was at this point, though, that the superhero began to take on an immunological function in defense of the city-as-village against corrupt officials and bandits. As the city grows, plant-like, from out of the earth, it captures the superhero the way a plant uses chlorophyll to capture sunlight as its primary energy source.

For by the time of Dashiell Hammett's *Maltese Falcon*, the rationalistic cosmopolis is up and running, a completely urban wilderness of skyscrapers and cable cars, where Hammett's noir hero, Sam Spade, has become the immunological protagonist whose task it is to keep beings out of ancient myth from ever creeping back in (precisely those beings that flourished in the festivals and rituals of the ancient agricultural village compound). The city, by this point, has grown and evolved, and along with it, captured the superhero as its primary defense mechanism.

With Robert E. Howard's Conan the Barbarian, however, the Culture Industry–radio, film, and press--generated as the bread and circuses for these masses is rejected altogether by a man who preferred his rural native Texas to the big city. Conan is always on the outside of the metropolis, never (except on rare occasions) within it or captured by it, and would just as soon see it dismantled into ruins.

Thus, with the exception of European forerunners, like Captain Nemo or H. Rider Haggard's Allan Quatermain, the superhero actually finds his origins in the Western United States, unfolding his various organs in an embryogenetic process that took place in locations like Los Angeles, San Francisco, Texas and, with Edgar Rice Burroughs, Arizona. There is apparently something essentially Western about him–expansive, like its great skies, and jaggedly powerful, like its granite cliffs and mountains serrated against the blue horizons. Indeed, the power of the sharpened rock or flint stone seems to be embedded within him, for as a visual signifier, he is powerfully contoured, just like a stone age weapon.

With comic strips and comic books, on the other hand, New York begins to extract him from the pulps and graft him into its architecture, where his cells become bonded and merged with the rectangular bricks and steel girders of its skyscrapers to become a sort of interior consciousness of the city itself. New York was, after all–and still is, for the most part--the center of the publishing industry and so comics emerged out of its newspapers like appendages sprouting from some rare and exotic animal. New York is a city in need of an immune system if ever there was one: we have seen how it was the task of the Fantastic Four to keep the city from being captured and closed down by the ancient metaphysical systems of the mythical age. The modern cosmopolis is an open one, both ontologically and physically speaking, and it must be kept open: naked to the sky and without protection against astral invasions. Attacks can–and historically now, have–come from all directions and upon all planes–both physical and metaphysical--and so it is the job of the New York superhero to keep the metabolism of its coded flows, with all its glowing signifiers, in perpetual circulation.

With James Bond, we reached massive proportions and saw the apotheosis of the superhero as a planetary being, viral in essence rather than immunological, as Bond was sent like a spore across the globe, infecting all native sign regimes with capitalist genes wherever he went. No superhero was ever larger or covered a more vast geographical terrain than James Bond.

And then, with Mad Max, the lights of civilization went out altogether: the hero came unplugged from the cities once again as he had been in the beginning–like Tarzan–and reverted to the status of a pure nomad moving across the flat spaces of vast Australian outback without goal or purpose. Indeed, Max is the hero who has come unplugged from all urban structures whatsoever, and regards them all with post-urban skepticism. He is strictly a hero stuck in permanent survival mode.

With the paranoia of Fox Mulder, the entire planet hovers on the verge of invasion by alien species from above–lacking immunological macrospheres to protect it–who are intent upon colonizing it and rewriting the Book of Genesis with their production of alien-human hybrids.

And now, with cable television shows like *The Walking Dead*, there are no heroes anymore at all, but only survivors.

Thus, the arc of our narrative has traced the evolution of civilization in an imaginary vision from its inception to its apocalypse. Today's heroes–on shows like *True Detective* or *Dexter*–have something unsettling about them and make one very nervous: they have come unglued somehow from the civilized order, and seem to suggest an age of exurban migrations to come, planetary refugees, perhaps–frightening, amoral beings, looking out only for themselves and on the move as the sea waters rise and the global temperatures heat up. With a planet of survivors and refugees from catastrophes on the way, then, the Age of the Superhero will soon be a thing of the past–a mediatic phenomenon only--something remembered with a fond nostalgia, perhaps, the way one remembers the days of radio or television as the dominant media.

We have, of course, yet to see what sorts of creatures the new medium of the Internet, together with all its digital gadgets will spawn, but by the looks of it, the likelihood is that the nature of these heroes–as both Breaking Bad and The Walking Dead indicate–will not be immunological at all, but rather more like Mad Max characters who are simply existing in survival mode after some planetary trauma has rendered civilization null and void.

Nowadays, in the Age of Catastrophe and the New Media Invasion, it is Everyman for himself.

Endnotes

Captain Nemo

1. Peter Sloterdijk, *In the World Interior of Capital* (Cambridge, UK: Polity Press, 2013), 40ff.

2. Ibid.

3. Gilles Deleuze and Felix Guattari, *A Thousand Plateaus* (University of Minnesota Press: 1987), 351ff.

Tarzan, Lord of the Apes

4. Although this is true only if we ignore Dr. Jekyll's ability to transform into his sinister counterpart Mr. Hyde, and the Invisible Man's ability to render himself transparent (that this is, indeed, a superpower is confirmed by the fact that it is Sue Storm's primary ability as a member of the Fantastic Four). These characters, however, belong more to the category of super villains than superheroes, for the super villain was invented *before* the superhero and heralds the latter's advent.

5. In the Tibetan epic of *Gesar of Ling*, for instance, the superhero is born when a god descends from the heavens riding on horseback and gives to Gesar's mother a drink that has been mixed with peacock feathers. The feathers identify him with the bird and the heavens, while the mother herself is actually a nagi, or serpent queen, dredged up from the depths of the ocean by Padma Sambhava precisely for the purpose of giving birth to the superhero Gesar. In the *Shanameh*, for comparison, the great hero Rostam is born from the union of his father Zal, who was raised from infancy by the simurgh, a mythical bird, and Rudabeh, who is descended from the serpent king Azhi Zohakk. The resulting heroes, both Gesar and Rostam, thus unite the powers of the sky father and the earth mother.

6. The plot of Burroughs' 1918 novel *The Land That Time Forgot* should be considered in light of this point, for it recounts the story of a soldier who, during World War I captures a German U-boat and accidentally discovers a hitherto unknown continent which the natives call Caspak, where dinosaurs coexist with Paleolithic human beings. Eventually, the Germans recapture their U-boat and leave the narrator, Tyler Bowen (note the Joycean homophone for "bone" or even "bow and arrow"), stranded upon Caspak with his girlfriend Lys. By the novel's conclusion the two have traded in their clothes for leopard skins and their guns for bow and arrows and have regressed to a Paleolithic way of life (or equally, Adam and Eve in the garden). The novel is actually a rather prescient forecasting of the coming descent of twentieth century Western civilization into an increasingly tribal way of life. Its imagery is also strikingly similar to the imagery in the opening chapters of *Finnegans Wake*, which begins with Vico's Heroic Age of tribal man who wears animal skins and hunts great beasts. Also note the rather synchronicitous fact of the West's retrieval of ancient dragons out of Heroic Age narratives like *Beowulf* through the discovery

of dinosaur fossils at just about the time that the ancient superhero of oral-tribal epics is beginning to resurface in the vestments of popular literature. In *The Land That Time Forgot*, the image of the German U-boat firing its machine guns at giant Plesiosaurs is exactly isomorphic to Paul Klee's painting *Sinbad the Sailor*, in which the Arabian hero is shown battling a sea monster.

Dinosaurs make their first appearance in a narrative, by the way, in Jules Verne's *Journey to the Center of the Earth* (1864) itself a retrieval of the mythical night sea journey of the solar hero to the underworld, where he normally encounters dragons, serpents or giant monsters. Hence, the mythic appropriateness of the novel's protagonists stumbling upon battling dinosaurs at the earth's core, a symbolic underworld.

7. The human mind, that is, as a culture forming and symbol making type of consciousness. In the world of physical anthropology, such mythic structures can be found all over the place, if one digs deeply enough. For instance, in naming the three million year old Australopithecine forebear of the hominids "Lucy" (after the Beatles' song "Lucy in the Sky With Diamonds" which happened to be playing on the radio during the dig) there is a tacit (though unconscious) recognition of Gnostic structures, for "lucy" means "light" and hence implies that the Australopithecine who is about to diverge from the apes and follow the evolutionary chreode that will lead to the advent of human beings contains a spark of divine fallen light within it, like gold in a sunken Spanish galleon awaiting rediscovery by divers. The name "Tarzan," too, as Burroughs points out in his novel, means the "white one," for Tarzan is hairless and white-skinned by contrast with the apes which raise him. The color white can also be read as being identical with "light."

8. The panther skin loincloth links him with the night sky, for the symbolism of the pelt of the spotted panther (or leopard) is universally associated with the stars of the nighttime sky. In Egypt,

for instance, the priests who performed the ceremony known as The Opening of the Mouth–in which a ritual instrument shaped like the Big Dipper is touched to the mouth of the mummy in order to resurrect it from the dead and confer upon it the ability to speak magical intonations that will protect it against evil demons in the afterlife–wear the spotted panther skin to signify the stars of the northern circumpolar constellations (such as the Big Dipper) that were known as the "Deathless Ones" where the souls of the dead were thought to ascend. Thus, the panther skin loin cloth of Tarzan connects him with the dark, lunar, chthonic cults of the night sky and the realm of the Mothers.

In the Chinese poetry cycle known as *Eighteen Songs of a Nomad Flute*, moreover, many of the Hun nomads who are shown invading a Chinese city in order to abduct Lady Wen-Chi are wearing panther skins in the form of saddles or quivers for their arrows or else as some other bodily adornment. Thus, the panther skin was apparently also linked with the world of the nomad, as is also the case in the Georgian national epic known as *The Man in the Panther Skin*.

Tarzan's hunting knife, furthermore, suggests the fact known to physical anthropologists that as the apes evolved over time into humans, they gradually lost their fangs, while at about the same time, (i.e. amongst *Homo habilis*) the first stone tools were being made. Knives were a typical part of these ancient Oldowan tool assemblages. And so the knife, a la McLuhan, becomes an extension of teeth. Tarzan's hunting knife is iconic, for he always has it with him, just as John Carter always has his sword (symbolic of the sun's cutting solar rays).

9. Irwin Porges, *Edgar Rice Burroughs: the Man Who Created Tarzan* (Brigham Young University Press, 1975), 220.

10. Gilles Deleuze and Felix Guattari, *A Thousand Plateaus*, (University of Minnesota Press: 1987), 351ff.

11. For a brief, but thorough, glimpse into the world of the nomad, one could do no better than to read the Chinese poetry cycle known as *Eighteen Songs of a Nomad Flute: The Story of Lady Wen-Chi*, which tells of the historical episode of the abduction of Lady Wen-Chi from her palace during the Han Dynasty around 195 A.D. The opening painting shows the city under siege by nomads, but the following cycle of paintings and poems shows the life of Lady Wen-Chi as she struggles to adapt to life on the smooth surfaces of the plains occupied by the nomadic Huns over a period of twelve years. It is notable that during this twelve year period, almost nothing at all happens beyond her giving birth to two children, for the world of the nomad exists *outside of history*. History is a function of the cultural metabolism of cities, but the nomads are locked into a historyless world of changeless landscapes and endlessly cycling seasons. When the Lady returns to her city, the final painting of the cycle shows the city as a bustle of activity (i.e. striated space) amongst merchants and craftsmen who are engaged in the processes of evolving and shaping culture, and hence, history.

12. In Johnston McCulley's Zorro novels, for instance, the primary villains *are* the Law, for Zorro's fight is against the authorities of the pueblo of la Reina de Los Angeles.

13. See William Irwin Thompson's *The American Replacement of Nature* on "the spatialization of time" in Disneyland. This is also evident in the opening pages of Nathanael West's 1939 novel *The Day of the Locust*.

14. Robert M. Fogelson, *The Fragmented Metropolis: Los Angeles, 1850-1930* (University of California Press, 1993), 21.

15. Ibid., 10.

16. Marc A. Ouaknin, *Mysteries of the Alphabet* (Abbeville Press, 1999), 185.

17. Georges Dumezil, *Mitra-Varuna: An Essay on Two Indo-European Representations of Sovereignty* (Boston, MA: Zone Books, 1990).

18. H.P. Lovecraft's 1933 short story "The Thing on the Doorstep" provides us with a good example of the Hydraic Ego, for the story concerns a man named Edward Derby whose body is gradually taken over by the astral spirit of Ephraim Waite, a man who had previously transmigrated into his daughter Asenath's body, whom Edward Derby had married. The story is recounted by Derby's friend, who tells of certain unsettling episodes of meeting with Derby when he no longer seemed to be himself but *some other person*. This other person is Asenath's father Ephraim; Derby realizes that his wife has been taken over by this man and so murders her and buries the body in his cellar. But then Derby realizes that his consciousness is being swapped, for Waite pushes him out of his own body so that he comes to occupy the dead body of his murdered wife Asenath, while Ephraim Waite takes over Edward's body. Edward meanwhile, having taken up residence in the dead wife's body, forces his way up from the cellar and drags his rotting body to visit his friend and insist that his friend must kill the man who had formerly been himself, Edward Derby. Hence, the "Thing" on the doorstep is the rotting body of Asenath with Edward's displaced

consciousness inside it. Ephraim Waite's astral personality which is able to take over the bodies and minds of other people is not that far away from a superhero persona like Zorro who emerges to displace the consciousness and idiosyncratic trademarks of the personality of Don Diego. Lovecraft explores similar themes in his 1935 short story "The Shadow Out of Time," in which ancient god-like beings are able to temporarily assume control of the human personality. (These beings are even closer to superheroes, since they are archetypal and transpersonal). David Lynch's 1997 film *Lost Highway*, by the way, is perhaps the ultimate reworking of this myth of the unstable self-identity which is pushed aside by an astral spirit.

The Maltese Falcon *and the Cosmology of San Francisco*

19. Gray Brechin, *Imperial San Francisco: Urban Power, Earthly Ruin*. (Berkeley, CA: University of California Press, 2001), 50.

20. Ibid., 51.

21. Ibid., 65.

22. John David Ebert, *Celluloid Heroes & Mechanical Dragons: Film as the Mythology of Electronic Society* (New Zealand: Cybereditions, 2005), 145-47.

23. Leonard Shlain, *The Alphabet vs. The Goddess: the Conflict Between Word and Image* (NY: Penguin Books, 1999).

24. Robert Graves, *The White Goddess: A Historical Grammar of Poetic Myth* (NY: Farrar, Straus & Giroux, 1975).

Flash Gordon

25. Peter Sloterdijk, *In the World Interior of Capital* (UK: Polity Books, 2013), 43.

The Fantastic Four

26. Martin Heidegger, *Contributions to Philosophy (of the Event)*, (Indiana University Press, 2012),24-25.

27. Martin Heidegger, *Poetry, Language, Thought* (NY: Harper Perennial, 1975), 141-159.

28. Mircea Eliade, *A History of Religious Ideas, Volume I* (University of Chicago Press, 1978), 200-203.

29. Boris Groys, *Art Power* (MIT Press: 2008), 101ff.

Spider-Man

30. Jean Gebser, *The Ever-Present Origin* (Ohio University Press, 1985), 191ff.

31. Ibid., 205ff.

32. Ibid., 215ff.

33. John Colarusso, ed. *Nart Sagas from the Caucasus* (Princeton University Press, 2002), 17ff.

James Bond

34. Daniel Biebuyck and Kahombo C. Mateene, eds. *The Mwindo Epic from the Banyanga* (University of California Press, 1989).

35. D.T. Niane, *Sundiata: an Epic of Old Mali* (Pearson: 1995).

36. Walter Ong, "Literacy and Orality in Our Times." *Composition & Literature: Bridging the Gap.* Ed. Winifred Bryan Horner. (Chicago: University of Chicago Press, 1983), 130.

37. Ebert, John David. *Celluloid Heroes & Mechanical Dragons: Film as the Mythology of Electronic Society.* (New Zealand: Cybereditions, 2005), 147-48.

38. Valmiki. *Ramayana Book Three: The Forest.* Trans. Sheldon I. Pollock. (New York: New York University Press, 2006), 191.

Mad Max

39. Paul Virilio, *Speed and Politics* (Los Angeles, CA: Semiotexte, 2006), 40-41.

40. Michel Foucault, *Security, Territory, Population: Lectures at the College de France 1977-1978* (Palgrave Macmillan, 2004), 325-327.

41. Catherine Malabou, *Ontology of the Accident* (Cambridge, UK: Polity, 2012), 1ff.

42. Paul Virilio, *Desert Screen: War at the Speed of Light* (NY: Continuum, 2005), 7ff.

43. Heiner Muhlmann, *MSC: Maximal Stress Cooperation: the Driving Force of Cultures* (NY: Springer-Verlag, 2005).

www.ingramcontent.com/pod-product-compliance
Lightning Source LLC
Chambersburg PA
CBHW060512100426
42743CB00009B/1293